ADVANCE PRAISE

I read the book from start to finish in one sitting. I could not put it down. It made me laugh and it made me cry. Hyppo is an extraordinary young man who has endured tremendous tragedy – and yet has found the will to forgive those who murdered his family. Goodness radiates from him – and he attracts kind and generous people like a magnet. Everyone who reads this book will be inspired with hope for the future - and will want to help others.

Emma Sky OBE, Director, Yale World Fellows, Senior Fellow, Yale's Jackson Institute for Global Affairs

A Boy Called Hyppo is a testament to resilience in the face of severe challenges. Hyppolite Ntigurirwa begins with his unforgettable experiences as a young boy forced to endure the unimaginable horrors of the genocide against the Tutsi in Rwanda and its immediate aftermath. He describes his journey from a state of destitute poverty in a post-genocide displacement camp to the club-like halls of European and American universities, as well as the inspiring combination of force-of-will and generosity of strangers that fuelled it. Finally, he recounts improbable and astonishing transformation from a state of vengeance and despair to his growth into an agent of compassion and reconciliation. He delivers it all with a sense of humor, wonderment, and humanity that is sure to be an inspiration to any who reads it.

David Simon: Director of Genocide Studies Program. Director of Graduate Studies, African Studies Advisory Board member, Yale University

In *A Boy Called Hyppo* Ntigurirwa undertakes a lucid, compelling and evocative journey into his past that will send shivers down your spine. That all trace of humanity vanished among the perpetrators of the genocide that targeted the Tutsi in Rwanda is indisputable. But it is also indisputable that the catastrophe that Ntigurirwa witnessed as a little boy did not destroy the strength of the human heart. With quiet elegance he shows with his example and in his encounters with others, how humanity triumphs over hate.

Pumla Gobodo-Madikizela, author of *A Human Being Died that Night: A South African Story of Forgiveness*

I have relayed this story to everyone I know – read it and meet a young leader who stands alongside Greta and Malala for courage, humanity and the ability to overcome tragedy and raise the human spirit. You will remember his name: Hyppolite.

Kate Robertson, Co-founder of One Young World

A BOY CALLED HYPPO

HYPPOLITE NTIGURIRWA
ANDREW CROFTS

ap

ISBN 9789493231122 (ebook)
ISBN 9789493231115 (paperback)

Copyright © Hyppolite Ntigurirwa 2021

Publisher: Amsterdam Publishers

info@amsterdampublishers.com

Book 1 in the series Genocide Against the Tutsi in Rwanda

Cover photo by Alyssa Palmqvist showing Hyppolite Ntigurirwa in his play "How Can You Say That"

1

VILLAGE LIFE

My father built our family hut so that he could marry my mother. Even a poor man has to have a house to take his bride to. It was nestled deep in the lush jungle foliage which coats the hills of Rwanda, close to the border of the Congo and Burundi, in a village called Gasharu. It is an area so inaccessible that most Rwandans would call it "the other side of the forest" or "the other end" or "the other Rwanda".

The floor was just the red earth, the walls a frame of wood that my father had chopped from the forest, filled in with a paste of mud and grass. He covered the roof with the bark which he stripped from banana trees. I was the youngest of their seven children and there was a space of about three years between each of us, but by the time I was born all nine of us were still living in that same hut. The closest to me was my brother, Protais, who was just three years older than me. Whenever he was not in school, we would be found together.

There were three rooms in the hut; one for my parents, one for the girls and one for Protais and me. The kitchen was outside among the trees. The toilet was a hole in the forest floor.

At night during the wet season, which stretches from September to April, the rains came in downpours and the water would find its way through the makeshift roof tiles. We would have to stand upright in the gaps between the streams of water, waiting for the storms to pass before we could lie down again to sleep on the damp ground. The goats didn't like the wet any more than we did and would make a fearful noise, keeping everyone else in the vicinity awake too. For the following day or two my father would spend his time trying to repair the holes before the next storm arrived.

We had one small goat at a time and some small chickens, all of which shared the house with us at night. The goats always had crazy characters and had to be attached to a post by a piece of rope to stop them running off. If you misjudged the length of the wire and you left any food within their reach, they would eat it, and we never had anything to spare. If they managed to reach anything in the night, we would have no breakfast in the morning and we would be working all day on empty stomachs. Or they would urinate on the food, which would make it inedible.

The goats were of limited value to anyone. To start with they took a long time to breed, and they didn't produce very much compost, but they provided us with something to sell if there was an emergency of any sort. Their meat was hard and not particularly pleasant to eat. Anyone who admitted that they drank goats' milk was considered to be out of their minds, and they hardly provided any anyway. But I loved being with them. They were my friends, although when they were naughty I would have to get cross with them and beat them, but I would talk to them as well. I felt that I understood their language.

The chickens were more useful and if we had a hen that my mother particularly wanted to breed from, and we didn't have a suitable cockerel of our own, it was one of my jobs to take her to a neighbour's cockerel to be mated.

My parents worked every waking hour to ensure that we all got something to eat each day, but they didn't always manage it. I was aware that some of the other children who I played football with sometimes had new clothes, or they would talk about having meat or rice or the little fish that came from Lake Kivu, things their mothers had bought in the public market, things which our mother couldn't afford. It's only later, when I think back, that I realise just how poor we must have been. I did not get to drink milk until I was a teenager, wear shoes or sleep on my own mattress until I was ten years old. No one in the family had any shoes, not even my parents, but that did not make us unusual in our village. When my sister was old enough to go into vocational training she finally got a pair and bought another pair for my mother. She couldn't do the same for my father because he had a disabled foot that nothing would fit.

Now I can see that it was a hard life, but I knew no different. I just wished I wasn't so hungry all the time, and I didn't like it when jigger fleas came up through the earth and burrowed into the skin of my bare feet to lay their eggs, eating into the flesh, causing constant pain which would stop me from sleeping. The more I scratched the more they hurt. Because I lay at night on a bed of grass, placed directly on the bare earth, and didn't have a mattress, I was always vulnerable to any creature that

3

cared to feast on my body while I slept. Nor did I like it when intestinal worms prospered on what little food there was in my stomach and made my rear end itch as they continued their journey back out into the world if I was able to find someone who could give me a pill. At the other end the lice would make my head itch so much I sometimes scratched myself raw.

Boys and girls in the village would sometimes spend whole days picking at one another's heads and crushing the lice and their eggs between their thumb nails. My father used to take time in the evenings to groom his children, showing his affection by cutting my toenails for me with a blade.

I felt ashamed to have these creatures living on me because it seemed like yet more evidence of how poor we were, although it was often more to do with me not washing myself properly. I wouldn't tell my mother until it was too late for her to do anything about it because they had spread too far. If I then complained to her about the pain and the itching she would tell me that I needed to learn to take better care of myself and that I should have told her when it first happened because there was nothing much she could do about it now, apart from trying to kill them by washing my clothes in hot water.

There were people in the area who did good business selling medicines for a variety of common complaints, but they had no training and would often promise whatever results they knew the customer was craving. Sometimes they did terrible damage by giving out the wrong drugs, just because that was all they had, and none of them possessed any medical knowledge. My mother would take care of most of our ailments. If I had a fever Mum would boil water and add eucalyptus leaves from the trees. She would then make me lean over the pot and inhale the steam with a blanket over my head.

Some people in the village were better off than us, but that just meant that they owned a cow or had a concrete floor to their house, or perhaps a few cans of oil so they could have light at night. The same fire that cooked our dinner would provide our light for the evening, once the sun had gone down at six o'clock, as it always does in a country that lies just below the equator. If we had a little oil we could fuel a lamp long enough to see our way to bed, but more often we used burning elephant grass from the fire as living torches. We tried to control the flames as we moved about but most of our clothes ended up with burn holes in them.

If I walked far enough I would pass houses that were made of proper bricks and had corrugated tin roofs to keep the water out and allow the family inside to sleep through the nights uninterrupted. I could only imagine how good that would be. These would be the families who would be able to pay me a few pennies to do chores for them as I grew bigger. Some of them were also the houses where plans were being laid for the destruction of my family and other families like mine, but I knew nothing of that when I was small.

The people who had more than us were the families who owned a little land on which they could grow enough food for themselves with something left over to take to market. If someone had space to grow a few extra coffee bushes then they seemed wealthy to us. My dad's family owned no land other than the patch that the hut stood on. We had a few things planted around the house that we could eat at certain times of the year, but that was all. We had to work for other people if we wanted to earn any money, but there were very few in our neighbourhood who could afford to pay anyone more than a few cents a day.

My dad had no education. I think he went to primary school, and he could read and write, but that was as far as he was allowed to go because he was a Tutsi. My mum had some training (septième supplémentaire), and she could speak a little French. My father's work was cutting trees from the forest for people who wanted to build houses. He worked with just an axe and a metal wedge and carried the wood on his head, walking barefoot. One of his feet was slightly deformed from birth, which meant that he always limped, but that never stopped him from working. Chopping trees and carrying wood is one of the hardest jobs in the world, and from the house we could often hear the sound of his axe smacking into the trunks for hour after hour. By the end of a long day he was sometimes so exhausted by his labours that he would vomit up blood. Some days, when we didn't have food, or any money to buy anything, I could see in his eyes how frustrated he was, although he would pretend that it was not a problem in order to protect us from worry.

None of this stopped my father dreaming, especially when he had been drinking too much banana beer at the end of a hard day. We would sometimes hear him on the other side of the hill, weaving his way home through the bush late at night and singing at the top of his voice about how one day he would be rich. I don't know where he got these songs from. Some of them were quite political, telling stories about how God had given some countries oil and other countries nothing. Although both of my parents were Catholics, and I think he believed in God, Dad did not go to church or worship as much as Mum did.

My sisters all seemed like grown-ups to me, and there was more than twenty years between my eldest sister, Appolonie, and me. By 1994 my fourth-eldest sister had already left home to be a maid for a distant family member who was not a Tutsi and had a government job in Kigali. People like us, who come from "the other Rwanda", have a reputation for being hard workers, so if someone has roots on that side of the forest they like to hire people from their own village, even if they themselves have moved on. She probably wouldn't have been paid much for her labour, but she would have had free board and lodging. It would have meant one less mouth for us to feed at home, so it would be seen as a favour that they were doing for our family. If she was ever able to take a few days off she would come home and would bring us clothes that her employers' children didn't need any more. Another of my sisters followed her to work for a different family, but she came home quite quickly because she didn't like the way she was treated.

Appolonie was being courted by Berchmas, a man who was well known for being part of an important local family. Whenever he came to call we had to rush around the village, trying to find chairs so that he didn't have to sit on the floor as we normally would. If it rained while he was with us the two of them would sit inside the house and we would make sure he was sheltered underneath an umbrella.

Berchmas and his family were Hutus, which meant that he had suffered a good deal of bullying, both at school and within his own family, for going out with a poor Tutsi girl, but he refused to give her up. It was a true love story, surviving against all the odds. His brother was a local leader, or mayor (then called burgomaster), and would remain the head of our Commune (District) even under the leadership that planned and executed the genocide against the Tutsi, so most of his family members obviously had reasons to be very against the idea of his brother being in a relationship with Appolonie and couldn't understand why Berchmas was so stubborn about giving her up.

She had not been able to go on to secondary education in school, even though she had passed the entrance exam three times, because her place was given to a Hutu kid. My parents, however, had somehow managed to find the money for Appolonie to take a professional course in order to become a primary school teacher. The money she earned from that job had allowed us to move from the hut I was born in and to build another, which was thatched with a thick grass rather than banana bark. Once again my dad bought some trees, cut them, and designed and built the house himself, with plans to build an even better one as soon as he could.

"You have told me my daughters are no good because they are not men," he sang now as he weaved his way home after a few beers, "but see what they are doing for me. They are building a house for me!"

Dad was very pleased when he had two boys after the arrival of my five sisters because before that the other men used to tease him, telling him that he was not a proper man if he could only produce girls He found it easier to express what he was thinking in song and when he had some beer in his belly.

"You used to say I am not a proper man," he would sing out, "but now I've got two boys and they will make me rich!"

Although for my brother, Protais, and me, it was funny to see him drunk, I could sense that my mum found his need to escape into drink frustrating, but I never saw them argue about it. Rwandan couples tend not to argue with one another in public or in front of their children. It is not part of our tradition. We loved it when he sang and I still remember many of the lyrics today. He had a wise proverb for every occasion too. It was him who taught me to dream big, although at that stage my biggest dream was that I would be given a pair of shoes that I could wear to church on a Sunday like the plastic sandals worn by some of the other children, or that I could have a new t-shirt and be able to eat meat like they sometimes did.

Even though there was nothing going on that would suggest that any of us would ever be able to improve the family's fortunes, Dad never stopped believing that things would get better. One year he planted about fifteen square metres of land by our house with coffee bushes. He had seen that coffee was the way that other farmers had generated profits, but of course we could never make more than a few dollars from such a tiny plot. He would also repair cooking pots for people for ten cents a time, cutting bits of metal to fit, and he would weave baskets from the small, supple branches of trees. Sometimes he even made beehives in the same way and taught me how to do it. When I put the hives in the trees around our house the bees came and we were able to make a very small amount of honey. We used smoke to try to stun the bees but I still ended up getting stung.

While Dad spent his days in the forest and looking for odd jobs he could do for neighbours, my mother worked on farms for any neighbours who owned land.

Once they had left school my sisters had to work, going with my mother to help her with the banana plantations or the rice fields which lay in a valley about two and half hours walk away. When I was very little, one of them would come back home in time to do some cooking while the others went to fetch more water.

Sometimes I would help my father carrying wood, but I had many other jobs to do around the house once everyone else was out at work or school. To fetch our water, I had to walk for forty-five minutes over the mountains to reach a communal supply, where I could fill up a jerry can in order to carry it all the way back on my head. In the summer, when there had been little rain, I had to pump hard to get anything, and it was never clean. The temptation was always to dawdle and take rests along the way, so if Mum was at home she would set a time limit.

"I am going to spit on this leaf," she would say, "and you must be back with the water before it has dried."

That same water would be used for washing any new or special clothes. For our everyday clothes we would just go down to the bottom of a nearby valley where some even dirtier, smellier waste water would lie, and wash them there, laying them out on the ground to dry.

School did not start until we were seven years old. In September 1994, when the new academic year started, I was going to be seven and would be able to start school myself, but until that day came round I had all these other duties, preparing for the meal and keeping the house safe. I started fetching water when I was five, and I would also have to find wood from the forest for the fire. Mum would allocate the day's chores before she went off in the morning. Because everyone else was older than me and therefore working or going to school, from the age of four I was often the only one at home during the day. So I had to make sure that we had enough wood for the fire and water for the cooking pot on the nights when we had something to eat.

Most of the time there was no food in the house during the day and we had to wait to see what my mother or my sisters brought home with them. If one of them brought home cassava or maize flour then we could make pasta. If we were lucky enough to have some beans then my mother would put them in water on the fire in the morning and would tell me to keep watch over them through the day, making sure that they didn't boil dry, adding a couple more cups of water if necessary.

Sometimes we would have nothing but sweet potatoes for a week, and I learnt that to cook them you did not need as much water as you did for beans. We also had avocado trees which would drop their fruit onto the ground. I had to wake up early to collect them in order to get there before the pigs or dogs.

I would wait with the food until the grown-ups got home and then we would eat and they would tell me I had done well, which made my heart swell with pride. Some days, however, the temptation was too great and I would just put a padlock on the door and go off looking for any of my friends who had also been left alone. During the day you would hear little else in the village other than the voices of children as we played football. Once our parents or siblings came home we had to ask their permission before we could go out and play on the road, but during the day we could please ourselves as long as we performed the chores that we had been given.

If I became too engrossed in the game, however, I would burn the food and there would be nothing for the family to eat that night. Then I would be in trouble and I would feel angry with myself and fearful of what my punishment might be. They were always careful to explain why I had earned a beating.

We respected our parents and would always obey them. They were strict with discipline. If we had done something very bad then neither of them would hesitate to beat us. We all knew that if we made a mistake we had to apologise and take whatever punishment they decided was appropriate.

When I worked as a shepherd, taking the goats into the forest, I knew that if I did not attend to what I was doing and allowed them to wander off they might get lost or they might eat someone else's crops and then I would have to expect to be punished. I understood all this, but still I would make mistakes now and then.

I also had to guard the goat and the chickens from the dogs that skulked around the huts in search of food. Dogs in the countryside were never kept in their owners' houses or tied up. They were always free to roam as they pleased, expected to hunt if they wanted any meat. No one could afford to waste meat on a dog and there is a limit to how many potatoes hungry carnivores are willing to eat before they go out looking for something to kill or something that has already been killed. Because they were constantly hungry and on the lookout for food, these animals could be savage and we would try to avoid them as much as possible, unless we knew them well, for fear of receiving a nasty bite. Sometimes, if we decided to go hunting small animals in the forest, one of my friends would bring his family's dog with him. We would run for hours as the hounds rushed ahead with their noses to the ground.

If we had eggs or small chicks then I also had to protect them from the hawks, which would always be waiting in the branches of the banana trees for an opportunity to pounce, and from the birds of prey which spent their days silently gliding in the skies above the forest, watching every tiny movement in the landscape below them. If I heard a warning cry from the mother hen I had to run to the rescue, making as much noise as I could to send the predator flapping away through the leaves. It was impossible to be constantly on guard but if I could keep half of the chicks alive then I would be praised.

Everything in the forest is being hunted by something and to keep the animals safe at night we would bring them all indoors with us, sharing the space. We also kept other small animals in the rooms with us. We called them mice, but they actually a kind of guinea pig, and they bred prolifically. I have been told that they were introduced to the country by the European colonialists to help combat the problems of malnutrition. They certainly helped provide us with meat, but they were also cute pets for me, all different colours, living loose in the house like they were our friends, and often gnawing holes in our clothes. They made funny, friendly little noises as they ran around. One of my jobs was to make sure that no dogs or cats managed to get into the house to kill them. I also had to find food for them, but there were some grasses (the

Dayflowers for example) which were poisonous to them. If I made a mistake like that they would all die. We could still eat them, but our breeding stock would then be depleted and it would be hard to start again. If I accidentally allowed a dog or a cat to get into the house during the days when I was in charge then they would kill them all and I would be in big trouble again because we would all be going hungry once more.

It was always annoying to be told I had to perform these tasks, but once I was eating the meal at the end of the day I would be glad that I had played my part in making it possible. It would usually be the only meal any of us had that day.

There is a famous Rwandan tale that in some families the mothers would "cook the bedcover" when there was no food. They would just boil up a bed cover, pretending to be cooking, hoping to get their children to sleep before they realised there wasn't going to be a meal. Our mother was too honest to try such a trick on us. If there was no food she would tell us, so that we didn't get our hopes up. Our meals were always cooked in one pot over the open fire. My parents would have their own plate, which they shared, and we would eat directly from a larger, traditional dish.

Although we didn't always have money for food, my mother was very aware of the importance of good nutrition and would take every opportunity to feed us the right things, even if they were in quantities too small to stave off the pangs of hunger. If she was working for a farmer who was growing a crop like potatoes and she knew that we had no food in the house, she would take some potatoes that the owners of the land considered to be not good enough for our dinner. When your children have nothing to eat you are forced to do things you would never otherwise dream of.

Mum was actually going to become a nun before she met Dad. She was training in a nunnery but they must have been very strict because they beat her when she refused to eat an avocado. Avocado trees were relatively new to Rwanda at the time, which seems strange now that they are to be found in almost every back yard. She didn't like them and the nuns beat her so she decided that perhaps the religious life was not for her and left. That was when she met my father. Now she has learnt to like avocados!

Her wages were around ten cents a day, not nearly enough to feed us all, particularly on the days when Dad had no customers wanting him to cut trees. Workers on these small farms are still paid very little today, probably less than a dollar a day, but it is not the fault of their employers, who would not be able to afford to hire anyone if they had to pay more. It is the way the system has worked for centuries.

None of these irritations, however, managed to dampen my underlying good spirits. If you had found your way down those muddy, unmade roads, over the deep ruts and round the potholes, through the crowded banana, mango, avocado, orange, eucalyptus, cassava and coffee plantations that surrounded and shaded each house, you would soon have collected an entourage of curious, barefooted children and I would probably have been at the front of the crowd. I would have been the cheekiest one; the one asking the questions, pushing close enough to greet and touch any interesting visitor. That lust for life is the only reason I can think of as to how I managed to survive the genocide against the Tutsi that was to befall us in 1994 and how I came to be standing on stages at some of the greatest universities in the world, telling my story.

Many nights we went to bed hungry, having eaten virtually nothing all day.

It is very hard to sleep when you have hunger pains, especially when you are lying on the hard ground and your skin is itching because of the invading parasites. There were also the night-time noises of insects and wild animals rustling through the undergrowth, setting the dogs off barking. Inside the house there would be the noises of the pet mice running around and rustling in the grass bedding.

The nights when he realised that there was nothing for his family to eat and that none of them had been paid by their employers were the only times I saw my dad sad. They were the only times when I couldn't see any hope in his eyes. He knew that, although we were all hungry, we were all still going to have to get up in the morning and go back to do another day of hard physical work, with the possibility that the same thing would happen again the following evening.

Even today I find it hard when I see people throwing away unwanted or uneaten food, remembering the times when the only food around our house might be one unripe banana on a tree. I doubt if it will ever be possible to get used to the idea that in many parts of the world people have more food than they can possibly eat.

In the morning, when the sun rose at six o'clock, the birds would start to cry out to one another and the village cockerels would crow proudly. There is one particular bird living in the forest that helped us to tell the time during the day because it would make a noise at precise, thirty-minute intervals, while the cockerels would mark the passing of each hour. It was useful since no one in the family owned a watch or a clock. The only other way to tell the time was if you heard a radio playing, otherwise we judged where we were in the day by how far we had got with our chores and by where the sun had got to in the sky.

Both of my parents knew that the secret of success was education and they insisted that all of us went to school for as long as we were allowed to. School was not free for any of us, but Mum and Dad would find the money somehow, even if it meant that we couldn't always eat. Because they were Tutsis, my sisters were not allowed to do any further education, it was the law, but our parents insisted they attended for as long as possible and they would check their school reports, punishing them if they were bad. We all knew the way the Tutsis were treated was unfair, but it was the way things had been for a long time so we just accepted it. We knew that this was not our time.

I knew that we were considered by many people to be "cockroaches" in need of extermination. To a large extent I accepted that this was just the way things were, that we were second-class citizens, but when I heard stories of Tutsis being beaten or even killed simply because of who they were, I knew that something was wrong. In the schools everyone knew that the Tutsi children were hardly going to be allowed to go on anywhere for further education so there was no need to worry about their academic progress. The teachers, who were mostly all Hutu, also knew that they could punish Tutsi children much more fiercely than Hutus, either making them kneel for extended periods of time, or beating them with sticks.

People talked about the situation openly and if anything ever went wrong in the village the Tutsis were always blamed. We heard grown-ups talking about "the Rwandan Patriotic Front" (RPF), a revolutionary political movement of Tutsis, and their army, the RPA, which was amassing over the border in countries like Uganda, threatening to invade and change the way things were done, but it all seemed a very long way away. My dad had a small radio that he would listen to if he could get hold of some batteries. Often, however, we went for several weeks without any news from the outside world.

Anyone who expressed any favourable views about the RPF was immediately beaten and killed, so we knew never to talk about it anywhere where we might be overheard, avoiding all political subjects. Some families were accused of sending their sons to join the rebel army and had to leave the village if they didn't want to be killed themselves. Even though I was just a child I could feel that something was wrong but there didn't seem to be anything any of us could do about it. We were just there, waiting to see what would happen.

Occasionally my cousin, Jovin, who was older than me and married with a child, would come to the house with other relatives and they would talk in hushed voices about what was going on. They were excited that the radio had told them the President had flown, under international pressure, to Tanzania to sign an agreement for power sharing with the RPF. They thought it meant that things would change for the better. I understood very little of what they were talking about, but it sounded like potentially good news. They had brought beer with them and they all drank together, their voices still low but their hopes high.

Everyone looked the same to me, and shared the same culture, religion and language across the village. Not all Hutus hated Tutsis. Most people tried to live in peace with their neighbours, regardless of their ethnic origins. Many Hutus and Tutsis that we knew had even intermarried. If the father was a Hutu then the children would be the same, but he would always be vulnerable to criticism from other Hutu men who saw it as an act of treachery. If the woman was a Hutu she lost that status as soon as she married a Tutsi man and was branded as an "accomplice". My parents were one of those couples. My mother and her parents had Hutu stamped on their identity cards, but because my father was a Tutsi that meant that all of us were the same as him

In late 1970s my mother took my father to meet a family friend who had been unable to attend their wedding. This friend was partisan of PARMEHUTU - The Party of the Hutu Emancipation Movement - (an extremist Hutu party that was founded in late 1950s). The visit seemed to go well but when my parents were getting ready to leave, my mum's friend took her aside.

"I can see that you have married a Tutsi!" he said. "Do you realise that one day, we will kill all the Tutsis and exterminate them and from Rwanda? Be ready for that time to come and your husband, your children and maybe you yourself will all be killed."

Such hate-filled words coming from someone she loved and respected made her shiver with fear, but all they could do was hope the prediction never came true.

Many of my parents' best friends in the village, however, were Hutu, including Felix and Clemence, a wonderful, caring and compassionate couple who were my godparents and lived just ten minutes' walk from us down the track. It was not unusual in the area to find Hutu and Tutsi families who were really close friends. Like most Hutus, Felix and Clemence had a little more land than us and were therefore better off, owning more livestock and even a small coffee and banana plantation. They used to brew a lot of banana beer and so sometimes, when my parents did the same, they would take their brew over to share with them for an evening. They always seemed to have a lot of food and sometimes, if we went with them, they would give my brother and me a portion of beans or some other treat.

If I did anything naughty while my parents were out at work, like throwing a stone at another child or being rude to an adult, it would be Felix or Clemence who would be called upon to discipline me. Any other parent in the village could punish me or other people's children because the parenting process was seen as a shared responsibility for the whole village. It didn't happen to me as often as it did with some other children because I was never a thief, apart perhaps for the occasional potato, and anyway my mother was pretty good at taking care of the disciplinary side of things herself. I respected them to the same degree that I respected my own parents.

Felix was one of the community leaders in our church in Mibirizi, which was about ten kilometres away, and he was well liked by everyone, so he had a lot of godchildren. All of them, except for me, were Hutus. If I missed a church service for any reason it would be Felix who would come to talk to me about it. If there was a feast at their house for a marriage or some other event I might get to sleep there for the night on a mattress. If they had a big wash day or they were brewing banana beer they would ask my family if I could help by fetching extra water for them, or wood for their fire. They made me feel like I was part of their family.

At the beginning of 1994, workers started to arrive in the area with picks and shovels, digging deep ditches in the hills. It wasn't long before all the children in the village had heard that there was something interesting happening and we gathered around the workmen to watch.

"What are these ditches for?" I asked one of the men.

"Public works," he said with a shrug.

I didn't think about the matter any further. People were always digging ditches for one reason or another. Some were used as toilets, others were to try to redirect the torrents of water that washed away the roads in the rainy season. It was grown-up work, nothing that we needed to worry about, so we just watched and giggled and nudged one another whenever one of the men said something funny. It did not for one moment occur to me that I was watching them dig my family's graves.

Sometime in February 1994 my brother, Protais, my youngest sister, Laurence, and I found some neighbours' children stealing sweet potatoes from our garden. These were children who we looked upon as our friends, who we played football with. When we challenged them they told us that it didn't matter because in a few days all the Tutsis would be killed and so anything we owned would belong to them anyway. They said they knew this because they had heard it on the radio. Because we seldom got to listen to the radio I hadn't heard all the broadcasts which were coming out, inciting all Hutus to "do their duty" and to kill Tutsis and anyone who supported them.

My friends' words were scary, but I simply couldn't believe that it was true. I could imagine that there might be some outside force that was threatening to travel to our village and attack people, but I certainly didn't imagine for a moment that the potential killers were already there, living alongside us. I believed that Mum and Dad would protect us because I knew how hard they always worked to look after us.

I knew nothing about the outside world beyond our village and the surrounding hills. I had been no further than the distance my bare feet could carry me. I had seen no soldiers or guns, no towns or paved roads or houses taller than one storey. There were no newspapers or photographs to show me what the rest of the world looked like, and no televisions because there was no power, even if anyone could have afforded to buy one. I did not see my first television until I was twelve years old. Very few cars or lorries ever made it down those tracks because in the rainy season it was too muddy and in the dry season the potholes were too deep. And what would there have been for them to come for anyway? Even today the arrival of a car in the village will bring a crowd out of the huts and trees and the children will stand around it, staring, reaching out to touch it in wonder. In many ways I had spent those first seven years as an innocent in the Garden of Eden, surrounded and shielded from the world by lush greenery and mist-covered mountain vistas.

Children all over the world say cruel, stupid and half-understood things to one another. Usually they are untrue, just ignorant bluster. I was too busy with my chores and with playing football whenever I had a spare moment, to spend too much time considering the implications of what they were telling me, until I woke up on 7th April and heard the sounds of surrounding homes being attacked, and the warning shouts from other members of my family.

2

KILL THE COCKROACHES

The night before, while I had been playing football with my friends in the road, the sunset had seemed to last much longer than usual, turning almost the entire sky reddish. It is something that everyone in the village recalls to this day, and at the time was seen by the elders as being a very bad omen. That same night the President's plane was shot out of the sky on the way back from a meeting of regional Heads of States that had taken place in Tanzania on 6th April 1994, which made the men in my world feel cautiously hopeful. A peace agreement between the RPF and the former government had actually been signed in August 1993. The plane had crashed into his palace gardens, killing everyone on board including the President himself and the President of Burundi, who had flown back from the meeting with him. These high level political developments were so far from my childhood world amongst the trees of the forest that it is hard to imagine how there could have been any connection at all.

My parents had come home late and didn't turn their radio on, allowing us to live in blissful ignorance for a few hours more. It was strange but that night the clouds turned a bright red as the sun set, almost the colour of blood. Although I knew nothing of what was happening on the other side of the mountains, it felt like there was something ominous in the air, a warning of some sort.

My cousin, Jovin, was normally a jovial man, full of jokes and smiles, always throwing me up in the air and making me screech with a mixture of fear and joy. He used to wake up very early every morning, ready and eager to tackle each new day. He liked to listen to the news on the radio, so he was one of the first people to hear what was happening and to realise that we were now all in danger.

The hatred which many people felt for us because we were Tutsis was now going to boil over and it was impossible to gauge what would happen next. The radio station was urging all Hutus to kill us immediately, all of us, and anyone who tried to protect us. If they didn't do their duty, and quickly, then the Rwandan Patriotic Army (RPA), who they always referred to as "the cockroaches" by the media, would soon be invading, with our help, and we would conquer and enslave them, as they believed we had done in the past.

He ran to our house and there was no smile on his face as he burst through the door. He did not stop to talk to me or lift me up, going straight to the grown-ups. Normally grown-ups would not have talked about things in front of the children that would make us fearful, but that morning there was no time for that. If anything they needed to make us fearful for our lives so that we would understand how serious the situation was and how hard we must now concentrate if we wanted to survive.

"It's time to go into exile," he told my father. "We are not safe here."

"Where are we going to go?" my mother asked. "We have nowhere to go."

"No one here will kill us," my father said, trying to calm the situation, "these are our neighbours. The killers are somewhere else. Let's wait and see what happens next."

"No," Jovin insisted, "we need to go."

At that moment Berchmas, Appolonie's Hutu boyfriend arrived, looking equally frightened.

"Something very bad is happening," he told Appolonie. "You have to come with me, so I can protect you."

Trusting the man she loved she went with him. My parents did not protest. It meant there was one less person for them to worry about, even though we did not know what fate might lie in store for her with Berchmas's Hutu family.

Another relative arrived with more news. I tried to listen and make sense of their words as they all discussed what they should do but this time they shooed us outside, not wanting to scare us with whatever tales he had to tell. It was too late; I could see the fear on their faces and hear it in their voices. There was a dark feeling in the air and it was impossible to work out what we should do to make ourselves safe.

"Go and put your clothes on," Dad told us eventually. "And pick up anything that is easy to carry."

"We need to split up," Mum told Dad. "It will be easier for us to hide. I will go with the girls; you take the boys to Felix and Clemence."

Mum and my sisters hurried away and we had no idea where they were going, what was going to happen to them or whether we would ever see them again. There was no time for any of us to pack anything; we just left with the clothes we were wearing, although I noticed that Dad had picked up his axe and the wedge that he used to make his living. He hid them in the plantation as we ran through the trees to my godparents' house, bent low, hoping that no one would see where we were going. I don't know if he did that because he planned to retrieve them when things calmed down and he went back to work, or whether he wanted to deprive whoever came to ransack our house of any more weapons that they could use against us.

My heart was thumping in my chest, my eyes wide with fright as I tried to take everything in, alert for any sign of danger, any flicker of movement which might signal that the attackers were close.

Felix and Clemence received us as warmly as ever, but it was obvious from the speed with which they told all three of us to hide under their beds, that they knew they were taking a risk by sheltering us. It was a good hiding place from the point of view of people passing by outside, but if anyone had come in to search the house they would have found us in seconds.

"Our lives are in danger," Dad explained. "So we have to hide here."

"Why are we in danger?" I wanted to know.

"Be quiet," my brother hissed. "The Hutus want to kill us because we are Tutsis."

I waited for my father to tell him off for making up something so frightening, but he said nothing. Maybe he hadn't wanted to put it in words himself, but he couldn't deny that it was true. I felt myself trembling uncontrollably and saw that both of them were the same.

"Which people are the Hutus?" I demanded. "Who wants to kill us?"

They didn't answer so I named all the people I could think of and each time my father answered, "No, they are Tutsis."

Eventually I got to Felix and Clemence.

"They are Hutu," he replied.

"So why don't they want to kill us?"

"Because they are our friends."

I was about to protest that I was not aware of having any enemies, but I could tell I was wearing my father down with my constant questions so I fell silent. None of it made any sense to me.

There were noises outside now as well as shouting. It sounded like building work but I knew it wasn't. I didn't realise until later that it was the sound of Tutsi houses being set alight and destroyed. They had started with the richer Tutsis, the teachers and people who worked in the local hospital, the ones with education who had brick houses full of possessions which the killers could steal. The plan was to start killing the people at the top and then work down to ordinary people like us. But there weren't many rich people in our area so it would not take long before they were all gone and we, the men and boys, would be next in line for execution.

Once darkness had fallen my godparents called us out to stretch our limbs and have something to eat. We weren't hungry and we talked in whispers, trying to think of better hiding places than just being under the bed. It was decided that Dad would hide in a ditch just outside the house, where the bananas had been placed for ripening in preparation for brewing. Once he was in the ditch they would cover him with the fruit, making sure that he was completely hidden but still able to breathe.

Protais and me they told to get under the upturned umuvure, a large canoe-shaped bowl which they used for making the beer. It was standing upside down in their hut, acting as a seat until it was needed for the juicing of the bananas, when it would be turned the other way up.

It was cramped and airless inside the bowl but we didn't argue, just obeyed them, not knowing that it was going to become our permanent home for the next few days. Once under it, it was impossible to move or stretch our muscles and so soon we were both suffering from painful cramps.

There was no option other than enduring the pain in silence. It was also impossible to come out to relieve ourselves. It was very cold as we clung to one another through the night and Protais grew worried as he felt a spreading patch of warmth as I wet myself, fearful that the stench of urine would give us away next time someone came into the hut.

By the time morning came I was in intense pain and terrified of what would happen next. We could hear clearly when several of the Hutu killers pushed their way into my godparents' house, loudly announcing that they knew Felix and Clemence were friendly with Tutsis and demanding to know where we were.

"How can they still be alive?" they yelled at Felix. "You should have been helping us to kill the cockroaches."

I clung tightly to Protais and I could feel that he too was trembling with fear. Peeking through a crack in the umuvure all I could see were the bloodied spears, clubs, knives and machetes which they held in their fists, ready to strike down any Tutsi they might be able to root out of hiding. The umuvure lurched as they sat themselves down on it uninvited. One of them had a list of names, which he started to read out, of people who had already been slaughtered. I knew nearly all of them. They were all local people and some of them were our relatives and friends.

I also recognised the voices of the killers; they were all men who lived around us, men who used to buy wood from my father and drink with him in the evenings after work and whose children I had played football with on the road and gone hunting with in the forest. They were people I would have said were our friends, who would have laughed at my father's drunken singing.

I still couldn't believe they were going to actually kill us. They might beat us, I reasoned, but surely nothing more. People couldn't just kill whoever they wanted, could they? If that was true how could we feel safe ever again?

"These are the people we are still looking for!" The killer continued reading from the list and then I heard our names. They were actually looking for us personally so that they could kill us with those machetes which were resting against the umuvure, inches from our trembling bodies.

"What is that terrible stink of piss?" one of the men asked. "Where is it coming from?" I felt Protais's fingers tighten their grip on my arm.

"The toilet ditch is outside," Clemence replied. "So I don't know what it could be. Maybe it is the leftover smell of the beer."

"Search the house again!" the man with the list commanded, maintaining his position on the umuvure as the others made a great deal of noise as they overturned everything else. It didn't take them long to look everywhere and I was certain that any minute we would be exposed to the light and air, and to the blows of their clubs. I wanted to cry out with fear but Protais held onto me so tightly that not even a whimper escaped.

After searching the house and making a few more threats, they left. I wondered if it was a trick and they were all just standing around, waiting for us to give ourselves away. They had made it clear that they would be back, so we still couldn't move from our hiding place.

We remained under the umuvure for several days, although I lost count of how many, being unable to tell night from day and having no way to judge the passing of time when I couldn't see the sun. The killers came back several times, each time angrier, louder and more threatening in their demands for information but still never thinking of turning over the umuvure. I guess it never occurred to them that anyone could survive in such a small space. If they had found us they would have chopped us to pieces there and then. They would have had to because they had said they would and it would have seemed like weakness for them to show mercy. They would have killed Felix and Clemence as well, for giving us shelter, as an example to all other Hutus who failed to carry out their killing duties as instructed.

It was like an act of God that they never looked under that bowl and I try to have an umuvure in every house that I live in, for luck.

Once we were sure that the killers had gone my brother and I would exchange whispers, speculating on who they had been. Later my godparents would confirm for us who the men had been. We often heard the adults talking about what was happening, describing what they had seen or what they had heard from others. We learnt that there were roadblocks all around the village, where people had to show their papers. If their papers were stamped "Tutsi", as ours were, then they would be killed there and then and their bodies would be thrown over the side of the road and down into the mass graves that were forming in the valleys below. The same would happen to anyone who refused to show their papers, or was suspected of having forged new ones.

Everyone had a horror story to tell of people who had been hacked to pieces and then left to die, others who had the tendons cut in their legs so they couldn't run away and could be dispatched later, at the convenience of the killers. We heard about things being done to women and girls that I didn't understand, beyond knowing that even telling the stories made the grown-ups weep. No one was safe, from old people to small babies, they wanted to kill everyone who had the word Tutsi on their identity card, and anyone else who tried to protect them or refused to join in the killing when ordered. I couldn't understand any of it. All I understood was that I, and everyone I knew and loved, was in enormous and immediate danger.

We stayed with my godparents for several days. Whenever they heard that a group of killers was approaching they would knock on the top of the umuvure and we would know that we had to stay entirely still and silent until the danger had passed. Felix made a point of sitting on top of us before they came in. Each time they pushed their way into the house, shouting and intimidating, I expected that this time they would think to look underneath it.

Each evening, as it became dark, Felix would let us out and Clemence would have prepared some food outside in the kitchen. None of us could relax, every sound making us jump and fall silent, straining to hear, constantly ready to run back to our hiding place, our godparents desperately trying to hurry us along with whatever we were trying to eat.

My godparents were obviously terrified we would be found out and our courage never lasted for more than ten minutes before we were ready to hide again. It didn't give us much time to eat but we had hardly any appetite anyway. It is impossible to think about eating when your head is filled with a thousand questions, every one of them terrifying, when all your senses are straining to catch a sign of danger. I would take one mouthful and then struggle to swallow it.

Most of the time was taken up with them telling us the news of the day, which was always terrible, just a catalogue of more people we knew who had been murdered and whose houses had been burned down.

Later, once we were back under the umuvure and everyone was asleep, the hunger would return and I would regret that I hadn't been able to swallow some food while I had the opportunity. Each morning, when the noises and the voices returned, the need for food would be forgotten once again as fear tightened its grip on our stomachs.

3

SEARCHING FOR SANCTUARY

About a week later, when we came out for our food in the evening, we noticed that the sky had turned orange in the direction of our house. The sound of pounding feet sent us scurrying back towards our hiding place, emerging a few moments later when my godparents' son, Michel, came in, breathlessly reporting that it was our home, the one that Dad had built with his own hands, which was now burning.

"You cannot stay in the ditch much longer," they told Dad. "The killers are coming by more and more often and they will notice that the bananas have ripened and are ready for brewing. They will wonder why we are not doing it."

"Where should I go?" Dad asked.

"You could go to the church," Felix suggested. "Many other people are sheltering there."

The idea of being safely within the stone walls of a church, a sacred place that we believed the killers would surely not dare to attack, was attractive.

"I can come with you," Michel told him. "We need to wait until it is raining. They are less likely to be out hunting if it is wet."

They thought that it would be better if we didn't travel together. Since we had survived this long under the umuvure it was decided that Dad would go ahead alone and we would remain in our hiding place a little longer. The prospect of being separated from both our parents was frightening, but we didn't argue. We trusted that the grown-ups knew best, and we still had Felix and Clemence to look after us. The prospect of leaving the house and running through the bush, where there were hunting parties all around, was even more terrifying than staying under the umuvure.

The following night there was a huge storm and all human sounds were drowned out by the crash of rain on the canopy of foliage. The thick clouds blocked out the light of the moon and the killers all stayed indoors to drink and laugh and celebrate the success of their campaign so far, boasting about how many cockroaches they had killed and how many more they would eventually catch.

Michel and Dad disappeared into the darkness to start the ten-kilometre walk across the muddy hills to Mibirizi, travelling along steep, slippery footpaths on the edges of ravines that would mean almost certain death if they stumbled and fell, avoiding every sign of human habitation, alert for the sound of drunken laughter or shouts between hunters. Protais and I remained in our hiding place, now having no idea where any other members of our family might be, or whether any of them were still alive.

The killers were becoming increasingly frustrated at not being able to find us and returned to the house repeatedly over the following days. If they had found us they would undoubtedly have forced my godparents to kill us with their own hands, as an extra punishment before being killed themselves. We heard stories of exactly this happening to other families.

A few days after our father had left, they decided it had become too dangerous for us to stay any longer and it was now time for us to go to the church as well. Clemence volunteered to take us herself, setting out early in the morning, before the sun had risen and the killers had woken up and returned to their hunting.

Because it was April it was still the rainy season, which meant that the crops were tall and the undergrowth was thick, affording us a lot of cover as we moved cautiously from one hiding place to another. If it had been later in the year, during the dry season, or after the crops were harvested, many more small children like us would have died during those months because it would have been harder for us to hide.

This was the first time that we had ventured outside my godparents' house since the killings began and the sights we saw were chilling, confirming all the stories that we had overheard being whispered about. Everywhere we looked there were bodies, many of them dismembered and hacked to pieces. There were people of every age, from babies to the elderly, lying where they fell or piled up in heaps.

There were as many women and girls as there were men and boys, and many of them had been terribly mutilated before being killed. Some of the bodies had been collected and tossed into the ditches that we had seen being dug a few weeks before, others had been flung over the sides of the mountains, catching on the rocks and trees on the way down, hanging like litter, or landing on others below, forming mass open graves. The smell of death was everywhere, making us shake with fear. I was terrified to think that the bodies of my parents and sisters could be lying in any of these piles and I would never be able to find them. I finally woke up to the fact that everything I had been hearing was real and true. They intended to kill every one of us and at any moment we might be caught and it would be my brains that would be spilled out into the mud.

As we came into the church, a place which had always seemed like a cool, quiet haven of tranquillity, we were greeted by a seething mass of people. Later we discovered that there were literally thousands of people sheltering in the building at that time. There were people sitting or lying everywhere with not an inch of space between them. We picked our way through the crowd, searching for familiar faces, overwhelmed by the stench of blood and faeces and sounds of crying.

Eventually we found Dad and the first thing I noticed was that there were tears in his eyes, as if he had been crying and was now trying to hold it back for our sake. The next thing was the gaunt look of starvation on his face, his eyes and bones shockingly prominent in his sunken cheeks. He probably hadn't eaten a single morsel of food since leaving the banana ditch a few days previously. In an attempt to quell the hunger pains he had made a rope from old cloth and had tied it tightly around his stomach. He kept coughing uncontrollably. I also found my best childhood friend, Jean Pierre, who was badly wounded and later died from those wounds. He and I used to plan together how we would go to school and grow up to become leaders. His mother also had wounds from machetes and spears all over the body and his father and only sister had been killed. His mother survived and had to live with the trauma and the pain of those wounds until she died in 2020.

The horrors that happened in that church, and in many other sites around Rwanda, have been well documented in the media and in other books on the subject. I do not want to force my family to have to re-live them yet again if they are reading these pages. The message that I am wanting this book to carry out to the world is one of forgiveness and reconciliation.

4

THE SOUND OF MACHETES

Having killed as many people as they could catch at the church the killers were soon fanning out into the bush in small hunting parties, shouting out to one another as they rooted us out, murdering everyone they managed to get hold of. I was shaking with fear as I tried to curl myself into the smallest of balls, like a foetus as I listened to the sound of the machetes. Even with all the noise of the men crashing through the bush and their shouting and the screaming of their victims I heard a small, familiar sound through it all. It was the sound of my father coughing and I knew they had heard it too.

Once I realised that Dad was dead and that there was nothing I could do for him, I scurried back into the church, which had now fallen quiet. I just had to work out the best ways to stay alive for the next few days, or hours, or even minutes; where to go, what to say if someone challenged me, how to get something to eat or drink, how to get some rest. There was no time to think about the future and no time to cry over what had just happened. I had to survive.

The stench of blood and death was overwhelming. They had killed everyone they could catch, which was most of the people in the church that day. The piles of bodies had grown so high that some survivors had burrowed in amongst them in the hope that they would be taken for dead themselves. It was something I would do myself many times in the coming days when I could find no other place to hide. The killers, however, took their time going through those piles of bodies, dispatching anyone who might still be breathing at their leisure.

They had wanted to cause the Tutsis they captured alive as much humiliation as possible, ordering them to strip naked before being killed. Later I would discover that the discarded clothes were then taken and given to the killers' friends and families.

Assuming that the killers would not think to come back to the church now that it was full of nothing but dead bodies, I settled down as best I could and tried to sleep. When I woke at dawn I heard noises from a little way away. I crept back outside and peered through the bush to see whose voices I was hearing. It was a small group of local Tutsi refugees who had come out of hiding and wanted to pray. Unable to get into their church because of the piles of bodies around the doors they were making their way to the nearby school to hold a service, behaving for a few moments as if it was just another day.

I wanted to join them in this apparent return to normality and escape from the nightmare of the previous hours, even if it was only for a few moments, and I decided that I would be less conspicuous if I was in a crowd than if I was wandering around on my own looking scared. Now that I was alone I just looked like any other village child. I took a deep breath and walked over to mingle in with them, trying not to shake, joining the congregation that was raising its voices in worship.

It was like stepping into another world, as if none of the horror piled up outside actually existed, although everyone looked exhausted, thin and frightened. For a few minutes it was just another day on which to praise the Lord. I recognised one woman who had been in the church with us. One of her children had a deep machete cut in his head and later died.

Once the service was over I walked back out again as if I was just one of the locals. When I was sure that it was safe and no one was watching, I dived back into the bush and started on the long walk back to my godparents' house, trying to work out in my head which route would be the one where I was least likely to bump into any killers. I was truly on my own now and I did not know what else to do or where else to go.

On top of the terror that made every muscle in my body ache, I was now desperately hungry and thirsty. I knew that I had to find some water so I made my way to the edge of the Nyagataka River, which I had drunk from many times in the past.

I made my way down to the edge, excited at the thought of finally slaking my thirst. To my horror I saw that the river was now clogged with bodies as the currents pushed them to the side and they became tangled in the branches and weeds. The waters which usually ran fast and clear were thick and red with blood. I felt physically revolted and retched at the thought of having to touch them, but I had no choice. I had to drink or I would die of thirst. I crouched at the edge of the water and tried to push the bodies away, but they were so waterlogged they were too heavy for me to move.

The blood lay like oil in the water and I tried to clear it aside with my hands so that I could drink from between the slicks, but it didn't really work. More than twenty years later I can still remember the taste and smell of that water clearly. It still haunts my nightmares.

There seemed to be bodies lying everywhere on the route that I walked along that day, even more than I remembered from our journey to get there. They were on the sides of the roads, in the rivers and in the houses, and the mountain valleys echoed with the moans and screams of those who were not yet quite dead. As I got closer to Gasharu I started to recognise some of the corpses as friends and family, people that had been part of my daily life ever since I was born. Some were still clinging to the last few breaths of life, others had been chopped to pieces. Most of them had gaping wounds on their necks and heads like Dad. Many heads were entirely severed. Whenever I saw someone I loved I stopped to touch them, as if to say goodbye and to assure them that I was going to be dead like them soon.

There was nothing I could do to help them. All I could do was keep on walking, putting one foot in front of the other, fighting to keep control of the terror that gripped me and to fight the weakness of hunger which constantly tempted me to lie down and rest. If I gave in to that I didn't think I would ever get up again. I couldn't stop the tears from coming, thinking that soon it would be my brains that would be lying in the dust and my life would be over.

All the time I was alert for the sounds of killers' voices; my wide eyes darting from side to side, ready to hide at a second's notice.

When I finally reached the house, Mum and Protais were both there. I was shocked by how thin Mum looked, her face all bones and eyes, her limbs like sticks. We couldn't talk for long before we had to be hidden. Mum was hiding either under the bed or in the kitchen area. Protais and I went back under the umuvure. Most of the killers had moved on from the village, I was told, believing that all the Tutsis had been flushed out of the safe houses. They were now concentrating on searching the bush and places like churches and schools where they could find large numbers of victims in one place, so it was a little safer than it had been last time I was there, but not much. If we made one mistake and were seen by one person with bad intentions it would all be over.

5

BY THE LIGHT OF THE BONFIRE

Some nights, in order to give Felix and Clemence a break, my mother, Protais and I would creep through the bush in the dark and try to sleep in the burnt-out ruins of our old house.

The roof of the house, which had been thatched with grass, had completely gone, as had the wooden structure of the walls and windows. Only some of the mud bricks were still standing. On the floor we could see the charred bodies of the pet mice.

On one of these nights we heard the familiar sounds of killers shouting outside, a frightening mixture of anger and jubilation. Peering through holes in the walls, past the coffee bushes, we could see that they were rounding up many Tutsi women and children, bringing them to the front garden of a house a little way down on the other side of the track from ours. It was a house formerly owned by a well-known local Tutsi. The place was also known as 'kwa Mukandoli'. They had built a blockade on the road outside the house and had lit a fire. The flames were high, sending sparks up into the night sky and making eerie silhouettes of the scene being enacted in the garden.

There was a toilet ditch just a few yards from the hut and they were making all the victims line up along the edge. The fire was burning so wildly that we could see clearly that many of them were members of our family. They were all just waiting beside the pit for their turn to die. None of them were making any attempt to fight or run. Some of them were pleading to be killed quickly and some were crying. All of them seemed resigned to what was about to happen.

As they taunted and tortured them, postponing the final moments as if enjoying the process too much to want it to end, several of the killers pulled young girls out of the line and into the bushes around our house, away from the flickering light and heat of the flames. We could hear their screams as they were raped, begging to be killed, while the men shouted abuse at them, using really bad words, telling they were going to be killed anyway so they might as well enjoy themselves before they went to the grave, telling them they were going to "cut their sex off".

I had very little idea about what they were actually doing, I just knew that the words were very bad and the screams were of pure terror as well as pain. I hardly dared breathe for fear that I would give away our hiding place and then it would be our screams that would be silencing the insects and animals of the night. What could I possibly say to them to stop them from killing us? Would it do any good for me to say I was sorry for whatever it was I had done to make them want to kill us?

Suddenly the scene in the garden became a bloodbath as the killers decided they had delayed their gratification for long enough and smashed and slashed at the heads, necks and bodies of their prisoners with machetes, hammers and heavy clubs viciously studded with nails. They came up from behind, encircling them so that there was no hope of escape. Once they had finished with the women in the bushes they dragged their bodies back and threw them into the pit along with everyone else. There were so many victims that some did not fall directly into the ditch, so their bodies were kicked or thrown in, some of them still alive and writhing in agony.

Protais and I watched with our mother the last moments of many of the children we had played with all our lives. All three of us were sobbing silently and uncontrollably, all of us certain that this was going to be our time to die and we would be the next ones to be dragged out of hiding. We still cry today when we remember that night together and try to work out exactly what happened, but at the time we only talked about what we were going to do next to survive. It was too much for us to be able to put anything into words about what we had seen and what we were feeling.

Eventually the killers' frenzy died down, their blood lust apparently sated for another night. By the time the sun came up they had all disappeared back to their homes to sleep and only the bodies remained, some of them still moaning and writhing in agony as they waited for the blessed relief of death. We ran as fast as we could past the ditch and back to my godparents and to our all-too-familiar hiding places. Even from there we could still hear the screams and cries of the dying.

6

TAKEN INTO SLAVERY

For the next few weeks we remained in our hiding places in the house with no idea how long it would be before the nightmare ended. Once the majority of the Tutsi men in the area had been killed, however, the killers changed their plan, spreading the word that they were willing to let the remaining women and children live if they gave themselves up.

There were now some senior killers living in the area, the people who had organised the local people to do their work for them, and they needed a workforce of children to do things like carry water and wood for them, and women to do the cooking and washing and to provide sexual services. We didn't believe that we would survive much longer if we stayed in hiding so we took the risk of revealing ourselves, even though we could not be sure it wasn't a trick to lure us out, and at that moment we became their slaves. They told us we would be safe as long as we did what they told us. Any of the women who might have had thoughts of resisting the raping were told that if they did not do exactly as they were instructed both they and their children would be killed. How low does a person have to have been crushed for them to believe that surrendering to sexual slavery is the best option available to them?

We were allowed to stay in my godparents' house but each day our captors would come and fetch us and tell us what our jobs were going to be that day. They would divide us into groups for different tasks. I always wanted to be with Protais because we were like two parts of the same person. We had been living the same life and seeing all the same terrible things so I felt safe with him. But one day the killers put us into different groups. I walked across to be with him and one of our neighbours who was guarding us shouted at me to get into my own group, pushing me back with his spear. I could feel the sharpness of the blade against my skin and the anger on the man's face made me shake involuntarily as I obeyed his instruction.

My group went to fetch water and I was terrified that there was some ulterior motive for separating us and that I might never see Protais again. He wasn't there when we got back and I could hardly breathe until I saw his group returning and spotted him, still alive.

Each day that we were collected from the house I feared it to be for the last time. I expected to be killed, but I wasn't and each evening I found myself back with my godparents. Sometimes the killers gave us a little meat to eat, but I found it hard to swallow because I could see that the machetes they were using to cut it up were the same ones they used to kill and maim people. In the end, however, hunger would triumph and I would somehow manage to get the meat down into my stomach.

In a way I felt that I was protected from the rest of the world by the killers I was now working for. We were marched back and forth to the water supply in a line, with a killer at the front and another at the back, both of them armed with spears which were still stained with the blood of our friends and relatives. In a way it felt like they were guarding us from attack as much as keeping us under control. I think things were much worse for the women and the girls. I know that terrible things happened to my mother during that time but she has never spoken of them and I have never dared to ask.

As we walked back and forth on these missions we saw that the killings were still continuing. The piles of bodies were growing higher, the mass graves filling up and the stench was growing so strong it was impossible to escape it. Often I would see someone I recognised lying by the side of the road with their limbs hacked off or their head split open but still not dead, writhing and screaming in agony as they waited to bleed to death. All day long we would hear the noise of people hunting for fresh victims. Although the days were passing and we were not being killed I could see that if one of my captors ever became angry with me he would simply chop my head open and that would be the end of everything. I stayed quiet and obedient, always on the lookout for ways to survive another day.

Eventually Mum decided that it was time to become proactive once more in escaping from our captors. She told us that our chances of survival would be better if we split up once again. Although I didn't want to be separated from her I didn't argue. I was already experienced enough in the skills of survival to be able to see that she was right.

Protais and I had a much better chance of staying out of sight if we were travelling on our own.

We had heard of a refugee camp a couple of mountains away in the south-west of the country, bordering Congo. It was called Nyarushishi. We decided that Protais and I would try to get to the camp while our mother would remain a little longer with Felix and Clemence.

7

THE REFUGEE CAMP

I had no idea what a refugee camp would be like, but I didn't expect it to be much safer than hiding in the village. I had seen that people who thought they were safe because they were inside a church had been killed, so I didn't expect it to be the answer, but it seemed like a better option than continuing to be slaves to the Hutus, who could kill us at any moment on a whim.

We started walking; constantly stopping to hide from any sudden noise, fearful that anyone we met might decide to kill us since we were no longer of any use to them. Mum decided she would accompany us for the first few miles. I guess she wanted to ensure that we were heading in the right direction. None of us had eaten properly for weeks so we were not as strong as normal, all our energy coming from fear of the alternative. Now we had started out on the journey we had to complete it. We also had to work out the best route to avoid any roadblocks that the killers might have set up that we didn't yet know about.

Every time we heard the angry, excited cries of hunters as they pursued new prey we would dart into the thickest part of the bush, and I would remember how I had curled up in a ball and listened to Dad's final moments on Earth.

"Cockroaches there! Quick! Catch them! Kill them!" they would shout whenever they spotted anyone who they thought might be a Tutsi or a sympathiser, but each time they ran past us, chasing some other unfortunate.

In the tangled undergrowth we nearly always stumbled over more dead bodies or parts of bodies. We were all in a state of perpetual fear of everything. I was now afraid of the light as much as I was afraid of the dark, afraid of every tree in case there was someone hiding behind it, afraid of the water in the rivers because it had been poisoned with decaying corpses. There was nothing that we didn't fear. We had no idea whether we would arrive at a safe destination, but to go back would not be safe and nor would stopping to rest. We just had to keep going.

Eventually Mum decided she had gone as far as she could and should now turn back before the killers missed her. We both hugged her and then she walked away, not knowing if she would ever see us, her youngest children, again.

Now Protais and I were on our own once more and unsure which was the way to the camp, despite all the instructions Mum had drummed into us on the path. All the people who we had relied on for protection were gone. Our Dad was dead and we had no idea where our sisters were or whether our mother would make it back to the village alive. Our godparents could do nothing for us if we were not under their roof. They were the people who I had always gone to for comfort if I was sad or afraid, but now there was just the two of us and we had to work out what we should do next. There was no one to tell me what to do, no one to reassure me that soon the nightmare would be over and to give me hope for the future. We never had any real plan as to what to do to get away from the danger and the killing, we were just ready and willing to do whatever we could to stay alive for another hour, living in the moment.

Most of the time we remained under cover in the bush, but occasionally we had to pass through an exposed area, and it was while we were crossing one of these that a group of killers spotted us from the other side of the valley. They became very excited, making the whooping noises we had learnt to dread, and began to run in our direction, but we were nimble whenever the adrenaline kicked in and too far away for them to catch us.

Eventually we found Nyarushishi Camp, with the help of a man who we met on the way, who was travelling in the same direction and took mercy on two lost and frightened small boys. The camp stood on two facing hillsides. The whole area was covered in tents made from sheets of green or blue plastic and was home to eight thousand people in various stages of sickness and malnutrition. We went in search of someone who might seem like an official and were immediately greeted with suspicion and taken to be interrogated.

Only a few aid workers of International Committee of the Red Cross were trying to organise enough food, but failing. There were people cooking, the smoke from their fires snaking up into the sky and offering hope, but there was still hardly any food and no one could afford to share what they had with a small, hungry boy.

I could see French soldiers here and there, but still it didn't feel any more secure than the church had. They didn't look like they were ready or would be willing to fight off any attackers. There seemed no reason why the killers should not attack us here just as they had at the church and we would have no way of defending ourselves. It was not long before I realised that my fears were well founded.

"Where are you from?" our interrogators demanded when we first staggered in from the bush.

"The Parish of Mibirizi," we replied, and a woman known to be from the same parish was called to vouch that we were who we said we were.

She recognised us immediately. "Your sisters, Placidie and Odette, are also here," she told us. "They had given up all hope that you were still alive. I'll take you to them."

She led us through the sea of identical looking tents until she found the right one. Our sisters burst into tears at the sight of us, and for a few seconds Protais and I felt a rush of joy at seeing such familiar faces and finding that they were not dead, as we had assumed. But then the reality of our new situation sunk in. We had arrived in hell.

There were dead bodies lying everywhere and there was no sanitation, so human excrement added to the stench of death and the spread of diseases like typhoid, dysentery and cholera. I did not feel safe, either physically or emotionally, and I realised that I was going to have to continue concentrating on surviving for as long as I could.

Hundreds of people a day were dying all over the camp, not just from the killers, who were lying in wait in the surrounding bushes and tea plantations, ready to kill any refugees who ventured out of the camp in search for food, water and firewood, but also from every kind of disease.

Despite the death rate more and more people were pouring into the camp every day and it was impossible to tell if they were survivors or killers. People were pitching their tents on piles of corpses and everywhere you looked you saw people taking their final breaths, lying in the filth and stench of a humanitarian disaster.

The only water for everyone in the camp came from the stream running through the valley, between the two hillsides, but to get to the stream you had to join the crowds, stepping over the bodies of people who had been previously ambushed by killers. If the killers attacked while we were at the water's edge you would hear the screams and confusion spreading through the crowd and then the distinctive sounds of machetes chopping into bodies as they went from tent to tent, hacking indiscriminately. The French soldiers were never anywhere to be seen when these attacks took place. The whole camp would start to make a noise, a communal wailing that would spread across the hillsides and warn of the danger, but there was nowhere for us to run for safety because outside the camp there were more killers waiting in the trees for us with their vicious dogs straining at the leash.

In the long days spent sitting around the camp waiting for something good to happen I made some friends, as small children always do, and we spent most of our time sitting together or wandering amongst the tents, feeling hungry and afraid, on the lookout for any opportunity to eat, alert for danger. One of those friends died but two of them are still alive today and we are still in touch, having shared an experience that no one else who hasn't experienced it can hope to understand. We don't have to explain or describe anything to one another because we all know how it felt and remember the pain and the fear.

Sometimes the Red Cross would manage to get some medicines into the camp, but there was nowhere for the sick to be treated because there were only tents and bodies, and infection in the air and in the ground and on everyone's hands. In the end they set up a makeshift surgery amongst the trees, where the air was a little fresher. But if you walked past you could see everyone being treated, no matter whether it was for a machete wound or for dysentery, and you knew that the infections were still spreading. I don't believe that there are any good refugee camps anywhere in the world. Some may have better health facilities or enough for people to eat, but the sadness and frustration of people who have lost everything, and the lack of hope for the future must pervade them all.

Every few weeks, just when I thought the hunger pains were finally going to overwhelm and kill me, a few cars would arrive and would distribute food to us via the largely self-appointed camp leaders. Then there would be flour and rice cooking on every fire for a few hours, but once those supplies had been consumed the long days of hunger would start again. The first sight of those aid cars would bring a flash of joy, as would the moment when I actually got to have a few mouthfuls of cooked food, but then I would see someone that I knew dying from an infected machete cut, someone of my own age, and the sadness and fear would return as surely as the hunger pains.

I didn't question what was happening, as I might have done if I was an adult, I just accepted that this was my life, that it was what I deserved because I had been born a "cockroach", and that I simply had to keep on living it for as long as I could. I didn't think back to how life was in the village before the killings started, and I wasn't able to imagine a world outside the hills where people lived safely and had enough to eat and drink every day. I didn't blame anyone for what was happening, not even the killers or the dogs I had seen eating the flesh of my relatives, I just accepted that this was the way things were for our family.

I did not tell anyone in the family what had happened that day in the bush behind the church. In the chaos no one questioned where Dad might be, assuming he was in hiding somewhere or already dead and lying in some mass grave. I just couldn't bring myself to say the words that would describe my last few minutes with him, or to deal with the effect those words would have on my mother and the rest of the family.

The hunger pains were so great that I would steal out of the camp at night, risking being ambushed and killed, to search for sweet potatoes, cassava, yams or bananas from the surrounding fields. Almost everything had already been stripped away by hungry fingers, only sometimes some of the unripe fruit and vegetables remained. On the rare occasions when I managed to find something I would stuff it into my mouth without pealing or cleaning, devouring it raw, anything to try to quell the agony in my stomach.

These were the times when I often had to hide beneath piles of decomposing bodies in order to escape the attentions of passing gangs of killers, pretending to be dead myself as I lay amongst the rotting, stinking, urine and blood-soaked corpses. Sometimes I would have to stay there listening while they killed more people and added their bodies to the weight pressing down on me, threatening to suffocate me.

Often I saw packs of dogs eating the bodies while I starved, and I was reminded of the moment when I saw my father lying in the bush, just a broken shell of the man who used to sing when he was drunk and cut my toenails with a blade.

There was no escaping the spread of sickness in the camp and as the days passed I grew so weak from dysentery that in the end I did not even have the strength to brush away the flies that congregated around my eyes and mouth, sucking the last vestiges of moisture from my emaciated body. They were the same flies that were swarming over the piles of dead bodies and human excrement that lay all around and in the narrow gaps between the tents. I had constant diarrhoea if I ate anything, and my head ached so much I thought it would split open. I was just a collection of bones covered in skin.

Sometimes there would be a roll call of names of people who had been killed or who had disappeared from the camp and people would start wailing and crying again as they had the deaths of loved ones confirmed. I didn't make any sound. I just watched, waiting for an opportunity to find something to eat or somewhere to lie down and perhaps escape for a few minutes into sleep. I could hear all the sadness going on around me but for me there was no time to cry. I had to keep going.

8

RETURNING TO GASHARU

By the end of July we began to hear stories of the Rwandan Patriotic Army (RPA) returning from exile and marching through the country, putting an end to the killings and protecting the Tutsis who were still alive.

Being on the other side of the forest, in the far south-west of the country, only reachable by potholed mountain tracks, we were the last part of the country that they reached, but eventually they arrived. Some people, who still had enough strength left, went back to the village to find food which they could bring back to the camp for friends and family. They were dangerous missions because the RPA soldiers were very spread out across the whole country and were not able to guarantee protection to people who were walking alone in the bush. Groups of killers were still hiding out everywhere, angry at having been forced to retreat, fearful at the reprisals they might now have to face and attacking anyone who they found on their own. Some of the bravest, however, got through safely and returned with tales of how our village of Gasharu was now becoming safer because there were soldiers stationed nearby who were guarding it.

We wanted to go back, but the journey still seemed too daunting and I didn't feel that I had the strength for the long walk. We heard that there was little or no food to be had in Gasharu and we knew that we had no home to return to, just a burnt-out shell.

Back in the camp the soldiers seemed to be allowing the killers to escape into the Congo and the rage of the fleeing Hutus, who were streaming through the country and into our area in the south-west, intensified the violence and the danger. As other parts of Rwanda were being liberated, we had to endure a further four months of fear and hunger before the RPA managed to break through to the camp. By the time they got to us we were little more than walking skeletons, unable to do anything for ourselves. They made the camp more secure, but that meant our movements were even more limited and we couldn't even go outside the camp limits to scavenge scraps of food in the surrounding fields. By this time the French troops had also withdrawn from the camp.

The mass killings eventually abated with the RPA's arrival, but the hunger persisted and hardly any food made it through to us. The first goal was to get everyone who was able to walk back to their homes. The RPA divided the camp into sectors that represented different parts of the country and we were finally told that it was safe for those who lived in our area to go home. They gave us a few very basic provisions of rice and corn for the journey.

Messages began to travel back and forth as to who was still in the camp and who was now back in the village. My mother was back with Felix and Clemence when she learnt that Protais and I were still alive and they all came to look for us, with the help of soldiers. My second bout of dysentery had not cleared and I was the weakest I had ever been, so the walk back was the most treacherous and painful I had yet endured, but there seemed to be some hope now for the future. As well as my mother and Protais and myself, three of our sisters Laurence, Odette and Placidie had also made it back to the village.

Only later did we find out what had happened to Appolonie after she left the house with Berchmas on the day the genocide broke out. As they fled down the road towards Berchmas's family home she could see that people were already being killed and Tutsi houses were burning. When they reached his house he locked her in a room, where he hoped to keep her safe until the killings were over. Some Hutu neighbours were furious that he had brought a Tutsi woman into his home, but Berchmas managed to convince them that he was just keeping her there for his own pleasure and that they would kill her once he had had enough of her. They reluctantly accepted the story, but every time Berchmas was away from the house they would taunt and threaten her and she was always fearful that they would rape and kill her themselves, or hand her over to others. She could do nothing to defend herself because if she ran away she would lose Berchmas's protection completely and would almost certainly be caught and killed by other Hutus.

Because she had worked as a teacher she was suspected of being a spy and communicating with the RPF as their army prepared themselves to invade from beyond the borders of Rwanda. The closer the RPA came, the great the danger for my sister as Berchmas ran out of excuses to give his neighbours for keeping her alive.

Somehow he managed to persuade them to allow him to take Appolonie with them as they fled to Congo. There she was forced to live in a camp with the same exiled Hutus who had just committed genocide against her own people and were now even angrier with the Tutsis for defeating them and forcing them out of their own country, taking back the powers that they had lost nearly forty years before. They never stopped harassing and threatening her and accusing the Tutsis of murdering the Hutus who had remained in Rwanda. To this day she finds it hard to talk about the years she was forced to live that life in Congo, expecting to be killed or raped every day, not knowing if the rest of us were alive or dead, but if it had not been for her love affair with Berchmas she might not have survived the genocide at all.

The war followed them to Congo, continuing their hardships, and Appolonie fell pregnant, which gave Berchmas another excuse to give her persecutors as to why they shouldn't kill her. When the Red Cross eventually reached the refugee camps in Congo, Appolonie asked them to make enquiries about us.

"If they had come back and told me that you were all dead," she told me later, "then I would not have wanted to go on. I would have killed myself."

But the Red Cross told her that her mother and siblings were still alive. We were as surprised to find out that she had survived as she was to find out about us, and we kept communicating by letter as Appolonie worked on persuading the family to return to Rwanda. Because we could tell people that Berchmas had never participated in the genocide he was safe to return, but we couldn't offer them anywhere to live because although the government had rebuilt our destroyed house by then it was not big enough to take in another family. They managed to find a place in an orphanage centre and once they had returned they married and Appolonie gave birth to their second child. It is worrying that despite all the efforts that the government and Rwandans have since the end of the genocide to abolish these polluted identities of Hutu and Tutsi, there are still people who harbour the same prejudices and the same hatred which led to the genocide of 1994.

Despite everything we had been through it was beginning to look as if we had been luckier than many other families. We knew many people who had lost everyone. There were children without parents and women who had lost their husbands and fathers and all their children. There were people who had lost limbs and had huge machete scars on their heads, necks and shoulders, and there were many who had lost their minds as a result of their experiences. There was nothing unusual about our situation, so there was not going to be any sympathy or support forthcoming, we all just had to go back to our lives as best we could, hoping that the mental scars would heal as naturally as the physical ones.

Because my mother had lived through everything in the village, and knew a great deal about who had been responsible for the worst crimes, she was asked to be a local leader (conseiller), and to help with the compiling of information and the decisions about who should be punished for what they had done and who was showing true remorse. Our community had to be rebuilt and that meant that we had to find a way of feeling safe, both when walking out in the bush alone and when asleep in our house.

Sometimes she would go out on patrol with other leaders, making sure that everyone was safe, shouting warnings if they came across any groups of killers roaming in the mountains, but they had no weapons that they could have defended themselves with if they had been attacked. One night they were walking in a line when some killers jumped out at them. Mum was second in the line and the man ahead of her was killed. She managed to outrun them and hid. We were not able to find her for a whole day, which was frightening and brought back all the memories of the months we had been without her and fending for ourselves.

Being a leader took up all her time and she wasn't able to earn money by working in the neighbours' farms anymore, that sort of work was left to my sisters. She did the job for three or four years but eventually the threats she received became too much to bear and she announced that she was retiring.

Nyungwe is one of the biggest natural rainforests in the world, so it was not hard for killers who knew the area to mount raiding parties and come in from Congo to take over a hill, robbing and killing anyone who made the mistake of travelling unguarded across their territory. It took the authorities a long time to make the forest safe from these bandits because the soldiers did not know the area as well as they did.

This was the forest that stood between us and the rest of the world. It made even getting as far as Kigali and Butare a big problem for the people in Gasharu and similar villages, meaning that we couldn't take advantage of any of the opportunities that going to a big city can provide for young people. We were even more trapped in the primitive life of the forest than our ancestors had been, in times when they could walk in relative safety.

Sadly, my godfather, Felix, who had risked so much to protect us and who was responsible for the fact that we survived at all, ended up being imprisoned because he was reported to have given away the hiding place of another Tutsi, believing that the man he was talking to could be trusted. Felix sadly died in prison in 2018. One of his sons was also convicted of having robbed some Tutsi properties during the genocide. It was sometimes impossible to differentiate between the truly evil people who had deliberately planned and organised the genocide and who had forced people to take part, and those who simply became caught up in the madness and committed terrible acts in order to be part of the crowd and to protect themselves and their families from being denounced as Tutsi sympathisers.

To anyone who saw us at the time we returned to Gasharu, we must have looked as if we were still close to death. I remember one day I was walking along the road with my mother. There were a lot of people around and a Red Cross vehicle stopped beside us. A white woman got out and gave me a biscuit that contained vitamins or something. I must have struck her as a particularly needy case, or maybe I managed to make eye-contact with her and caught her attention. Now, whenever I meet people who were there that day, they tell me that they have read about me going abroad or seen pictures of me with white people and they tease me; "Your blood was always loved by white people, ever since you were a child!" And they remind me of that day and how I was singled out by the white woman.

The most urgent job was to rebuild houses for the people who were returning from the bush, the refugee camps or wherever else they had gone to hide, so that we had some shelter and security and could get on with our interrupted lives. No Tutsi houses had been spared in the rush to destroy all traces of our existence. The money for reconstruction was provided by a Survivors' Fund, (FARG), set up by the new government, who also decreed that two days a week people must help in the effort by undertaking voluntary work in their community, including the rebuilding of houses. Some of the villagers helped in good spirit, but there were some who were very resentful of the fact that there were any survivors at all, still believing that we were all supposed to be dead. Those who refused to help would be fined but the fines were only small amounts and some of the richer ones preferred to pay the money than help us.

Many of the killers who were found guilty for their crimes were made to do community service, which also included building the houses that they had destroyed. Men arrived from the local sector office carrying the necessary wood and tiles on their heads to restore our home. Everyone was given twenty-seven large metallic tiles. It seemed that grass roofs were now going to become a thing of the past. Everything else was restored to the way it had been before, with no other concessions to progress or modernity.

Apart for our father, the only one who hadn't made it back to the village by the end of the year was Appoline, (as opposed to my other sister, whose name was spelt Appolinie), who had been working as a maid for a Hutu family in Kigali. We assumed that the family had murdered her. Some months later, while we were sitting around the floor, having a family meal, there was a knock at the door and Appoline walked in. For a moment we thought we were looking at a ghost. It turned out that although she had been through a lot, she had survived. Great moments of joy like this were often followed by a deep sadness at the reminder that our father was gone and would never be reunited with any of us, and that we had lost so many cousins and friends and neighbours.

Several dozen soldiers who were looking after our village set up camp in a house opposite the local school, which was about a mile and half along the track from our home. I loved the soldiers because I felt protected by them, just as I had once felt protected by my father and the other men in our family. Like many other boys my age I loved the way they looked, so powerful in their uniforms with their guns and their boots and belts. They seemed invincible, just as the killers had seemed to me when they came with machetes and spears but much better, much smarter, much prouder because they had right and justice on their sides.

Although I didn't feel any hatred towards my childhood Hutu friends, I didn't feel close to them anymore and didn't want to play with them. Even when we played, I had too much caution. There was too much that I wanted to say to them but knew I couldn't. If I had once opened those floodgates, how would I ever have closed them again? So the soldiers became my new friends and I would go to see them every day both before and after school. I was fascinated by everything about them and spent as much time with them as I could, going on runs with them at five in the morning if I could wake up early enough, and as long as my feet weren't hurting too much from the jigger fleas I would be able to keep up with them once my strength had returned. Protais would come too, but it would be me who was constantly asking them questions, sharing their food at every opportunity, being the cheekiest one.

Most of the soldiers were the sons of Tutsis who had fled from Rwanda many years before and they had lived most of their lives in Uganda, training in the mountains, fighting to bring President Museveni to power. Now they were returning to bring peace to their own country. I loved listening to the songs they sang, some of which were very naughty and made us giggle, even though we didn't always understand what they meant. The other kids, particularly those from Hutu families, were frightened of them but we never were, even though they were such tall, imposing figures with their uniforms and guns, because we knew they were there to protect us from the bullies who wished us harm.

One morning Protais and I got up early in order to go running with the soldiers, as had become our habit. We were walking along one side of the valley on the way to their house when we heard a familiar hunting cry going up from the other side. It was a renegade group of killers on a hunting raid who had spotted us and saw the chance of some sport. Luckily we were fast enough to escape, but it meant that we didn't get to see the soldiers that day, and we were reminded that we could never completely let down our guard. I met one of those soldiers again recently and he told me that he remembered how they wondered what had happened to us that morning, and concluded that we must have overslept.

Without the protection of the soldiers we would never have survived. One day, about three years after the genocide had officially finished, the soldiers heard that a group of Hutu killers were coming over from the Congo to our village and they came to our rescue. There was a gunfight all around the house and the killers were defeated. If the soldiers hadn't been there the outcome would have been very different.

Another big contingent of soldiers was camped out near to our church, so after mass in the mornings we would join them. Some of the other kids would feel bold enough to come with us, unable to resist the lure of these exotic looking men, the music they played and the food which they would hand out to us if they were cooking. Once they got to know us well they would do things like give us meat at Christmas.

"Are you a survivor?" a soldier at the church, called Gatera, asked me one day.

"Yes," I replied, gesturing towards the church.

He was obviously deeply moved because he picked me up and hugged me, hitching his gun up onto his other shoulder, and I saw that he had tears in his eyes. I was surprised because I didn't imagine that a soldier would ever cry. Until then I had seen them as something more than human, super-humans maybe, but now I could see he was just a man with emotions like me. We became good friends that day and I would always go looking for him after the Sunday service, knowing that he would take time to play with me and would give me food. But a year or so later his group was moved somewhere else and I never heard from him again.

We had started to return to the church at Mibirizi as soon as it was safe because there was no other church in the area for us to worship at. It was hard to be in the building, remembering the sights that I had seen there with Dad. It was even harder to walk past the place where he had been killed, even after visiting it with Gatera. I did not yet have the strength to walk into the bush to visit the actual place on my own.

Many of those soldier friends are retired now and I sometimes see them working in security somewhere. I always go over and introduce myself and remind them of the ragged little barefoot boy who used to follow them around everywhere and who they were so kind to. They are always amazed to see how much my life has changed since then. I will always be grateful for the part they played in guarding me during those years and in providing me with positive role models at a time when I had more or less given up trusting anyone or hoping for anything good to come of my life.

9
___

STARTING SCHOOL

Even before we were back in a house of our own, I had reached the age when I would be allowed to start school. The school itself was still a very basic set of buildings. There was one classroom built with bricks but all the others were made from the same wood and mud as our homes. Football pitches and playgrounds around it had been carved from the mud and dust by the scuffing of generations of children's feet.

No child was allowed to start primary school until they were seven years old. Not everyone, however, knows exactly how old they are and many children like me were eager to start earlier, so they devised a test; if you could reach your right arm over the top of your head and touch your left ear then you passed. If you were not able to do that you were sent home and told to come back in a year. You were also not allowed to wear shoes. If you went to school in shoes your parents would be called in to answer questions. I suppose it was because they did not want the children from families who could not afford them to feel inferior to those who could.

Just because I was now a schoolboy did not mean that I could stop doing the chores at home, particularly as my father was now gone. I had to take a jerry can with me to school each morning and bring it home full of water in the evening. For a while we had some pigs and before leaving for school each morning it was my job to take them into the forest to look for things for them to eat. That meant that sometimes I would be late arriving at school, which meant that I would be beaten by the teacher. It made me unhappy to be in trouble, but the physical pain of the beatings was nothing compared to everything else I had been through.

Without Mum and Dad's earnings our need to bring home money to live was even greater and I would do whatever I could on the days when I was not at school to make a few extra pennies. On weekends I would walk over the mountains for hours in order to buy three big sticks of sugar cane, which would each be at least six feet long, for the equivalent of about one penny. I would then carry them all the way back home over the mountain. The journey would take a whole day and in the heat it was a heavy and unwieldy load. I would then chop them up and sell them one piece at a time, which would last about a week and end up with me making about half a penny's worth of profit.

One of the reasons I did it was because I loved to chew on sugar cane myself. It was the only tiny luxury we ever had. I never minded doing my chores, like walking to fetch water, if I occasionally had something sweet to dig my teeth into. I still have a taste for it today and buy it when I see it, which gives away the fact that I am still a village boy at heart, even if now I am usually sitting in a car when I eat it.

I always liked to take on jobs which allowed me to get out and about, to see as much of the world as my legs would allow, even though many of the paths out of Gasharu held terrible memories. It was impossible to walk past the places where I had witnessed people being struck down or seen piles of bodies, and sometimes even had to burrow under them in order to hide, without remembering. It was impossible to walk past a river without picturing the time when it was so clogged with bodies and blood I couldn't find an inch of clean water to drink.

The taste and the smell of human blood is something you never forget, and because I witnessed so much butchery I now find it emotionally hard to eat meat of any sort, however good it might taste. If I walk past a butcher's shop and glance in, the displays do not look like food to me, they look like murdered and dismembered bodies. In the months following the genocide all the mountains had that terrible smell as the corpses waited to be disposed of in a more dignified way. I didn't tell Mum, or anyone else in the family, how hard it was to travel amongst these memories because I didn't want them to tell me to stay home. What would be the point of that anyway? If I stayed home in the village there were even more ghosts to haunt me in every direction I looked. Whenever possible I would try to find someone that I could walk with, so that we could talk and laugh as we went, keeping our minds occupied in order to keep the memories out.

Once the army had restored order to the area they started to exhume the bodies from the mass graves where they had been dumped and the smell that rose in clouds and drifted across the landscape was different, now more like rotting fish. That aroma too has stayed with me ever since, even more painfully evocative than the smell of blood or the sound of machetes hacking through flesh and bone. But still I stood on the edges of those trenches, horrified but transfixed, along with so many other people, as the bodies of friends and relatives were disentangled from one another. That was a time for crying and hysteria and sometimes for people to hug the remains of their loved ones one last time, letting loose some of the hurt and pain which had been pent up for so long.

My mum had to be there when the bodies from the nearby pits were being identified because of her role as a local leader. I think she also hoped that she might come across my father, but that was virtually impossible as he had been killed some way from the village. We assume he was buried in one of the graves somewhere around the church, close to where he was killed, and it is thought that there are tens of thousands corpses there, so there was little chance of finding one person, especially as many had been eaten by animals and there were only bare bones left.

Many of the faces of the dead were still recognisable, even if they were distorted with screams and fear and starting to decompose, as were some of the clothes, even though they were dark with blood. Many of the people we knew wore more or less the same t-shirts all the time, so much part of their identity that their colours and patterns were as instantly recognisable as their faces. Desperate family members would gather at the side during these mass exhumations, hoping to find evidence of where their loved ones had fallen, and perhaps some clues as to how they had died. Many of them became traumatised when they found a loved one, and equally traumatised when they failed to find them and realised that they would never know the truth of what had happened.

So many bodies had been thrown into the rivers, drifting down to the lakes of Uganda, unrecognisable by the time they were washed up onto the shores, the remains buried hurriedly by strangers to avoid the spreading of diseases.

It was never good news. I suppose there was a part of me that hoped I would get one last chance to see my father's body, because when they eventually got round to digging up the mass graves at the church in 1996 I felt myself inexorably drawn back to watch, but it wasn't long before I realised it was impossible, there were just too many bodies. He was one of a million and his remains could be anywhere. At least I knew the exact time and place of his death, even if I didn't know what had happened to his body afterwards. How much was devoured by the dogs? Did the killers really come back and slice off his nose? Many people did not have even that much to cling to. They saw their friends and relatives dragged away, screaming, and had no idea what happened next, or possibly they only knew something had happened when they didn't come home from work one day.

At some point we inherited a cow from my mum's dad and one of the jobs I took on was to take cows that belonged to neighbours, along with our cow, across the mountains to the warm, salty thermal waters in order to wash them. Sometimes I was paid for the work and sometimes I did it for free, if the neighbour's shepherd wasn't available. I couldn't swim very well, but I could hang onto the tail of the cow as it swam in order to stay afloat. There were always a lot of people gathered around the edges of these waters, doing the same thing as me or looking for other ways to make a few pennies. Many of them were from the Congo. The first time that I did that the men at the water's edge told me that I needed to be very clean in order to be allowed into the water, despite the fact that I was about to wash off a muddy cow. Boys like me were not allowed to wear any clothes, we had to be naked.

"You have to be circumcised," they told me.

This was a shocking revelation. I certainly didn't like the idea, but if I didn't take the cow into the water and wash it thoroughly I wouldn't be paid when I got home, so I now had a problem.

"Okay," they said, when they saw how distressed I was, "this time we will take the cow in for you, but next time you have to do it yourself, so you have to get circumcised if you plan to come back."

It seemed like I did not have a choice. There were a number of Congolese people there who were set up to provide a circumcision service there and then, using a small piece of wire, like a tie from a plastic bag, to pinch the foreskin and then scissors and blades to do the cutting. Summoning all my courage, knowing that if I didn't do this I would not be paid, I agreed. The pain was indescribable. Afterwards they gave me two or three tablets. I had no idea what they were but I guess they were penicillin or something similar. Whatever it was, it didn't work because the wound quickly became infected and smelled very bad indeed. I was desperate to hide what had happened from my family because I was embarrassed and I also knew they would be worried.

The next week I went back again with a cow and looked for the man who had done the operation since he had told me to find him if there was any problem. He was nowhere to be seen. I explained to the other men that I couldn't go into the water because the wound had not healed.

"Okay," they said, "we'll take the cow in for you because you are now a man."

Once the pain had finally subsided and the infection had cleared up I felt very proud of myself for having undergone such an important rite of passage. I felt my dad would have been proud of me, since I was working so hard to provide for the family.

Whereas once I had longed for the day when I would be old enough to go to school, I didn't really want to do it anymore. I was feeling an anger growing inside me which I didn't know what to do with. Sitting in a classroom with a bunch of other children, learning about maths and reading, seemed like a waste of time after everything that I had seen and learnt about real life. I would talk to the soldiers about it and they all told me that I must go to school and that getting an education was the most important thing. They were the only advisers I had by then because my mother was too busy trying to put our family and home back together at the same time as attending to her duties as a local leader and my sisters were now all struggling with their own adult lives. So I took their advice and went to school because I wanted to please my new friends, but I remained very quiet in the classroom; in fact I remained silent. I had so much of importance in my head that I wanted to talk about, so many stories about what had happened to me that I wanted to tell people but which I knew they didn't want to hear, that I couldn't find the words to make normal conversation or become active and vocal in the classes.

It was hard to do the written work as well because there was no one at home to help me in the mornings, and I had chores to do anyway, and by the time I got back in the evenings it would be dark, so if we didn't have any oil for the lamp I would have to try to work by the firelight, which was hard when I was already tired from walking and carrying water.

I felt that I was much older than my classmates because of what I had been through, although many of them would have seen similar things and been through similar ordeals. I didn't care about what any of them were thinking, retreating instead into my own world. I would look at the teacher standing in front of us and imagine what they had been doing a few months before. Had they killed anyone that I knew? If I saw a drawing in red ink it would remind me of all the blood I had seen flowing. If I saw a cabbage I would be reminded of severed heads I had seen rolling away from their bodies. If we all made a noise, repeating the sound of a letter we were learning from the blackboard, it would remind me of the chants and cries that the killers would let out when they came hunting for us in the bush.

Everything I saw or heard seemed to bring back some terrible memory that I had put to the back of my mind during the months when I was concentrating on pure survival. The heat and noise of the voices of forty or so children in the classroom was oppressive and I often yearned to just get back outside into the quiet, wanting to go looking for my friends the soldiers or to be with Protais or alone with a goat or a pig in the forest.

Even though the genocide had officially ended, there were still dangers all around us. The soldiers would warn us sometimes that we should not sleep in the house at night because they would not be there to protect us and there were always rumours that groups of killers would be coming back over the border from Congo to attack whoever they could find.

"Sleep out in the bush," they warned us, "it will be much safer because there are not enough of us to guard every house."

My mother was able to find places during the day where the greenery was particularly thick, where we could hide from sight, curled up on the ground like animals. Although I understood that it was safer than staying in the house, where killers would know where to find us, being that exposed always reminded me of the bushes I had been hiding in on the day that I heard my dad being hacked to death. I had also been told many stories during my childhood, no doubt exaggerated through repetition and for dramatic effect, of the terrible poisonous snakes, some even with lamps for eyes, which ruled these areas, although I have to admit that in all the nights we slept outside I never saw any. The only time I had a really close encounter with a dangerous looking snake was when I was on my way to school and had to deviate into the bushes to relieve myself. I was squatting down, doing what I had to do, when I heard a rustling behind me and turned to see the snake heading towards me with his eyes fixed on me as if I was a small, tasty meal. I did not stay to finish my business.

We continued having to sleep out in the bush, or sometimes in the houses of friends, for the next five years. There was one night when we were sleeping out when a group of killers attacked the area and killed many of the leaders. If we had been at home my mum would definitely have been one of their targets and we would almost certainly have died with her. Because they couldn't find her they left a written note, telling her that they would be coming back to kill her because she was "sending their children to prison". She received many messages like that during those years.

The attacks by armed killers were not the only thing that we had to be afraid of. AIDS was also taking a terrible toll, particularly among women. The disease had already been present in the country for ten years by the time the genocide happened. The mass rapes and deliberate infecting of victims increased the spread during the years of chaos and because many of the people killed in the genocide had been medical professionals of one sort of another, the epidemic was able to spread even faster during the late nineties. We were already hungry and traumatised, and now we had the shadow of a killer disease hanging over us as well.

My mother was following my progress at school, just as she and my father had done with my sisters and brother, and I always had to show her my report card. Sometimes I would take it to show my godparents too. I had no expectation that going to school would do me any good because I had seen how everyone else in my family had had their educations curtailed at the end of primary school. I never said anything in class and didn't have any great interest in what we were being taught. I just did what I was told, listened to what the teacher was saying and took the exams when the time came. I thought no more about it.

The first time that the teacher read out the grades and my name was top of the class I couldn't stop the tears from coming. All the other students were applauding as I walked to the front of the class in a daze to collect my report. I simply didn't understand how that could be happening. It was a shock to me because I had always accepted that I was a "cockroach", someone who was sub-human and could never be as good or successful as a Hutu. If everything I had ever been told and everything I believed was true, how was it possible that I could come top of the class, doing better than all the Hutu children around me? Did this mean that no one could kill me now? It was a puzzle which I did not yet dare to talk about. Even though my confidence had been lifted and I could see a glimmer of hope in the future for the first time, I still didn't feel able to speak out. So I remained silent, concentrating on the things that the teachers were telling us and doing the work that was required of me. My grades continued to soar.

When I told my mother that I was top of the class she bought me a t-shirt as a reward. I felt that I actually had a value in the world for the first time.

10

GIVEN PERMISSION TO TELL MY STORY

Still, however, I did not speak out a lot in class. Still, I longed to be able to talk about the things I had seen and experienced and still I knew that others didn't want to hear about it. The pressure was building inside my head and the following year I had to move up to a new class, full of new people who knew even less about what I had lived through and I felt even more overwhelmed by the contents of my head. Suddenly my grades crashed and my young teacher took me to one side. He was from a Hutu family. His father had participated in the genocide and his family had fled to the Congo when the RPF took over, leaving him behind.

"Why don't you talk in class?" he asked. "I see that you were top of the class in the last semester and now you are fifteenth."

"I want to tell people my story," I said, finally allowing the tears and the emotions to flow. "I am completely full of sadness."

He listened patiently as I poured everything out and then, when I had run dry, he said, "So, what do you need to succeed again? What do you want to say?"

"I don't know," I shrugged.

"I have an idea," he said, after a few moments' thought. "Why don't we start a theatre club, then you can get up on stage and talk about whatever you want. You can tell everyone your story if you want to."

Soon after that he announced to the whole school that from now on there would a theatre club which would meet twice a week after lessons. Every two months we would put on a performance of anything we chose. He then took me aside and asked me if I would like to create a play around the things I wanted to say about people killing one another. I wrote a script for a one act play entitled "How Can You Say That?". Never, in my wildest dreams, could I have imagined that one day I would be performing the same play to an American audience in Boston.

Our families were not supportive of the idea, believing that we shouldn't be expected to work outside of normal class times. I expect they were also reluctant to have the whole horror story resurrected once more and old wounds opened up. I wasn't the only one who had found it difficult to talk; no one was talking about what had happened. Everyone wanted to believe that the hatred and the killing was an aberration that was now in the past and that we had nothing more to worry about. I refused, however, to be deterred, as did my teacher and the other children who had signed up for the theatre club. I surprised myself with my ability to write. We all loved performing and we all loved learning and talking about the arts. Our teacher helped us to refine the messages so that they were not too upsetting for people. We even put some jokes into the script and some dancing. We wanted to entertain people as well as to make them think.

We staged the play on a Sunday afternoon after church and many people came, not just everyone in the school but local leaders as well. The atmosphere was tense and I was very nervous, frightened that I had made a terrible mistake, but as soon as I stepped out onto the stage I found my nerves melting away. The words came naturally and I could feel that the audience was very quickly with us. Everyone loved it, laughing at some parts and crying at others. Suddenly we found that we were famous and I found that I had a voice once more. All the resistance from the families melted away, as if perhaps we had said out loud some of the things they too had been thinking. To finally be able to speak about some of the things that were going on in my head, and to see that people were listening and to hear them applauding at the end, was like having a weight lifted from my shoulders.

I went back to the top of the class and I was still there the following year. I am certain that discovering I could perform and communicate with people was a big part of that, but also the awareness that our family was beginning to restore and heal itself. There was still a war going on in Congo and the violence would frequently spill back over the borders, but at least we were able to speak about what had happened and how we felt about it. I re-established my relationship with my two best friends from the village, both of them Hutu children, and went back to playing football, just like we had in the days before the genocide began, despite the fact that so many of my other friends were now gone.

By the time I finished primary school I had started to ask deeper questions about why the genocide had happened at all and why such an intense hatred had been transferred down the generations, and why it had exploded in such terrible cruelty and violence. Like a typical boy I also wanted to know why I had to study so hard and why we had to be so poor. What sins had I committed to be punished like this? These were all things that I had simply taken for granted as a child but which I now wanted answers to. I must have driven the teachers mad with my endless questions.

Some children dream of becoming doctors or scientists, but I never had any dreams like that. All I wanted to do was to talk to people, but what had I got to say? How was I going to continue living this miserable life? When I thought back to my childhood I could see how poor it had been. What had I done as a small child to have to be so hungry all the time? I could see that I had not deserved all the things that had happened to me because I had done nothing wrong and the frustration started to grow inside me. I soon realised that none of the grown-ups that I was pestering had any answers to these questions either, and some of them became openly irritated with me, perhaps thinking that I was trying to catch them out and show them up as being ignorant. After a while I stopped expecting to find any answers or solutions, so as I changed from a child to a teenager I simply became deeply sad.

11

HIGH SCHOOL

The GSFAK High School that I went on to at the age of around thirteen was a lot further from home, sitting in an idyllic hillside position overlooking the waters and islands of the beautiful, peaceful Lake Kivu. So I was going to be a boarder, not a day pupil, and once I had got there I would stay for a whole three months at a time. I was excited at the thought of moving away from the village and surrounding mountains for the first time, but nervous too about what surprises the outside world might hold for me.

Arriving there for the first time the beauty of the lake, with the mountains in the background, took my breath away. I couldn't believe that this was the view I would be able to look at every day from virtually every window. It must be one of the most idyllic locations for a school anywhere in the world.

To get there at the start of each term involved a four-hour walk in order to reduce the costs of travel, with my luggage balanced on my head in the traditional African fashion, and then a long bus ride. The winding, bumpy roads to the school were still unmade and so if it was the rainy season we might be delayed a day or two on our way back and forth simply because the buses couldn't get through the mud.

I was not alone on these journeys; there were some other children from my village who had also managed to pass the exams to get into the same school. GSFAK (the letters stood for Groupe Scolaire Frank Adamson de Kibogora), had a good reputation, having been founded by the Free Methodist Church. The government had agreed to pay the school fees of children who had survived the genocide, which allowed my brother and me to be the first people in our family in living memory to go beyond the primary educational level.

On the national stage Paul Kagame, the leader of the RPA (Rwandan Patriotic Army, as it was now known), had become President, having been Vice President since the end of the genocide, and was instigating an ambitious plan to develop Rwanda into a "middle income country", which meant he was concentrating his efforts on developing healthcare and education programmes. His other aim was to eradicate the terms "Hutu" and "Tutsi" from everyday language and official use. From now on we were all "Rwandans", working together for a common cause. Although it is impossible to wipe out centuries of ill-feeling overnight simply by willing it to be so, it was an important step in helping us to recover from the atrocities of the previous few years and to feel some sense of optimism for the future.

Next to the school, but a little further up the mountain, was a private school, (IJW), for children who hadn't managed to pass the exams for High School but whose parents could afford to pay their fees. There was a fence between the two schools, but it didn't keep us apart, particularly if there were romances afoot.

The language used in the school was French, but I only knew a very few basic words like "bonjour", conjugation and the days of the week. Until then I had always spoken the local language of Kinyarwanda. I was not the only one starting at the school with this disadvantage, most of the rural children knew no French at all. Most of the teachers, however, were Congolese and had moved to Rwanda to escape the war. They all spoke French and none of them spoke Kinyarwanda, but once I understood them I realised they were very good teachers even though they didn't all have teaching qualifications. It was later said that some of them had forged or bought their degrees before leaving the Congo, but it didn't matter because we were the ones to benefit from their natural abilities. In my last year of primary they started teaching more French for students of the last three years, which gave me just enough to continue on to the next stage.

When we arrived, we were told that if we were caught speaking our own language we would be given a rusty old padlock to wear around our necks on a chain. We would then have to keep it on until we found someone else who was speaking Kinyarwanda, so that we could pass on the symbol of shame. It was a surprisingly effective way of motivating us to learn a new language. The quicker you could pick up French the quicker you could start learning and scoring high marks in class.

We also had to learn English. I think I had a natural talent for languages, so it wasn't a great problem for me. I didn't, however, find maths or physics so easy. I was also introduced to different sports and discovered that I was good at basketball, Karate and Taekwondo. I didn't like the sports that came too easily to me; I liked to work hard to master new skills.

On top of these school activities I was also learning how the modern world worked. I had never seen a movie or a television before and had no idea how they worked. In a hair salon near to the school gates I used electric clippers on my hair for the first time, which made me feel very sophisticated and grown up.

On Friday they showed us films, most of which were in English, and on Saturdays we watched football matches. For some reason movies didn't catch my imagination and I often used the time to sleep because I was working so hard to keep up with the curriculum that I was always tired. Often the movies they showed were about wars and fighting and I had no interest in reliving those experiences. I wanted to move away from the killing and the hate that I had known all through my childhood and learn about the good things of the world. Watching any non-fictional films about the outside world, even football matches from foreign countries, was like seeing a dream world. It was impossible to imagine that I would ever actually go to such places myself. None of the fictional stories seemed as vivid or dramatic as the reality that I had lived through; none of them conveyed the fear and exhaustion of being permanently hunted and knowing that so many people wanted to kill you and had been given permission to do so.

There was a little ritualistic bullying of new boys at the school, and if the bully was a Hutu he would use the fact that I was a Tutsi against me. But it was not enough to spoil the excitement of my new life for me. Being at school was fun. And now I was no longer hungry or thirsty or tortured by jigger fleas and lice.

The school provided meals and on top of that the traditional singing fishermen on the lake were always bringing to shore the little fish they scooped up in their nets during the night. They cooked the fish on the shoreline with cassava bread or pasta which they would have made in the morning, selling these snacks to us for almost nothing. My friends, some of whom had a little money, would also buy me cassava paste and bananas. The joy of always being able to satisfy any hunger cravings at a moment's notice was overwhelming.

Sometimes we would skip lessons – mainly maths in my case, because I hated it – to go swimming in the calm waters of the giant, silent lake and to eat afterwards. That was where I taught myself to swim. If the discipline master saw some students swimming when they should have been in classes, he would come down to the edge of the water and wait for us to return. We would then be in big trouble.

The fishermen's boats were a distinctive sight going out at twilight with their three hulls and the long, arched poles holding the nets. Their voices, singing in time to their paddling, echoed off the surrounding mountains, their lamps twinkling like stars across the dark water.

I always find that I gravitate towards people who are older than me, just like my soldier friends back in the village. It was the same at school, and one of my older friends introduced me to porn a bit earlier than most of the people in my class. It caught my attention and I watched it because it was interesting and I knew nothing about sex, but then it started to remind me of the things I had seen and heard as a child, the screams of the women when the men dragged them into the bushes, and I thought it was horrible and vowed not to watch it again. It made me feel like I was complicit in the sins of those men. Being a teenager, of course, with the normal teenage urges, I was tempted to try a few more times, but each time I was only able to watch a few minutes before I had to leave.

I loved everything about school life. I was popular and successful and learning about art and theatre as well as languages and sport, winning an award from the Ministry of Infrastructure for being the "most powerful poet" in the school for a poem I wrote about protecting the environment. My prize was thirty pounds, which meant that I could buy food for myself, and repay the generosity of my friends.

12

DECIDING TO BECOME A KILLER

During the second phase of high school, when I was fifteen, I was allocated to become a primary school teacher like my sister, which meant that I was going to have to switch to a new school, which was even further away from the village, another two hours' bus ride from the Lake Kivu school. To get there by bus each term was going to cost just over three pounds in English money, which was an amount I did not have and I knew my mother didn't have either. In fact we had no money at all. So, when I came home from high school for the last time I was convinced that it would be the end of my education simply because I did not have the bus fare to get to the next school.

I had never chosen to be a primary school teacher, it was just what they pointed me to when they saw my exam results, but at least it was a way to continue my education. I wasn't happy about it because I knew how little my sister had earned in the past. It was the lowest paying professional job in the country and the least respected. Up until then my teachers had been suggesting that I might do something like studying literature because I was good at languages.

I tried to get allocated to a different course but the school authorities told me I would need to go to Kigali to get a letter. I couldn't possibly find the money for a trip like that so I had no option other than to follow the course that was being mapped out for me, but I couldn't even do that unless I could find the bus fare to get to the school in the first place.

The National Fund for Survivors was helping students like me to afford school materials, which we would be given when we arrived at the school. They actually gave me the bus ticket but I used to go to my former school, GSFAK, to ask if I could stay there instead of going on an expensive journey. Despite all the good intentions and ambitious plans of the government things were hard in the whole country. There was widespread hunger and suffering all through the country, made worse by the political conflict and fighting which was going on in Congo.

Our family was particularly badly hit because my second eldest sister, Odette, who had married a soldier, had become sick (she died in 2005, leaving behind two children for us to look after. Her husband had died before her) and was in hospital and unable to work. We didn't have enough food or any money. We had nothing like goats or chickens that we could sell. Even my godparents were not sufficiently wealthy at that time to be able to offer enough help, and my friends the soldiers had left the area.

It was a terrible shock to find that in the real world nothing was changing for us. The killers might have gone, but the poverty, sickness and hunger remained, making it seem almost impossible that we would ever be able to escape into better lives. My place at the school was waiting for me, but if I wasn't able to get the money I needed to make the journey I knew they would not keep the place open indefinitely. I could see that, unless there was a miracle, the one opportunity I had to move forward in life would soon be closing.

To my mother and sisters, finishing my education early did not seem such a terrible thing because none of them had gone on to higher education and so they accepted it as the inevitable fate of families like ours. They could see that I was a sad boy, but there was nothing they could do or say to make me feel any better and they all had enough work and enough worries of their own to fill their time. My brother had gone on to a seminary school which was just three or four hours walking distance from the village, so he did not have to worry about travel expenses, and I missed his company. I felt very alone in the world, unable to see any path forward.

When you are a small child you are full of trust and you think everyone is good until they prove themselves to be otherwise. Even if you have not been through a traumatic experience, as I had, when you become a teenager you may well start to become politicised and that is when you learn how to hate and to bear grudges to those who have done you wrong in the past and who now seem to be standing in your way. It can also be the time when you may channel that hate and learn to be sexist and racist. Your changing hormones can take you to terrible places during those turbulent years. Trapped back in the village which had been the location for the shattering of all my childhood illusions, I could not think of anyone who could inspire me, give me hope or make me believe that I might be able to do something good or useful or interesting with my life.

A few months before I had believed that I was doing well in school and that I had a good future ahead, but now it had disappeared. Now I felt again how I had felt before I went to primary school and discovered that I could be top of the class. It seemed that I was a cockroach after all, that for the want of a bus fare I was never going to be allowed to fulfil my dreams. I felt that I had been de-humanised again.

So what was I going to do with my life if I couldn't get an education? All the anger that had built up inside me during my childhood, and which I had been able to channel into my various interests and activities in school, returned. I had been getting my revenge on the world by succeeding in life despite what all the killers, and the politicians behind them, had tried to do to me. The children of our neighbours, many of whom had been involved in the genocide, were still able to go to school, but I was back where I had started and there didn't seem to be anyone who could help me. If anything, it was worse because those years in school had opened my eyes to the possibilities of success and happiness and escape, all of which I now felt had been snatched away from me.

If they hadn't killed my dad then he would have been there to help me, or my older cousins like Jovin, but they had all been taken away from me and the anger at this continuing injustice was burning and growing inside me, hardening my young heart. I remembered how Dad used to dream that his children would get rich and make his life easy, and I could see no way that was going to happen now. Was I doomed to a life of disappointment and powerlessness, just like him?

In the mornings, having nothing better to do, I would walk slowly over the hills to the church. I took to spending my days in the bushes where I had heard my dad's last cough, not returning home until the evenings, knowing as I walked back that there would almost certainly be nothing for us to eat, and telling no one where I had been or what I had been doing.

Now there was no sign that anything terrible had ever happened amongst those bushes. The plants had continued to grow and the animals and birds continued with their lives, as they had probably been doing since before mankind ever arrived. I would lie face down on the ground for hours, invisible to passers-by, talking to him as if he was still there, asking him questions, feeling like we were having a conversation inside my head, crying all the tears that I had held back at the time. Sometimes it felt like I knew that he was crying too and sometimes there were long silences.

If some passer-by heard me crying and came to see if I needed help I would tell them I was looking for wood for my Mum and that I was just tired. If I became too hungry I would find a field and use a stick to dig up a sweet potato, which I would eat raw. Every day for several weeks I went back, wishing that I could be dead too, and eventually I came up with an answer to all the questions spinning around in my head.

If I could no longer take my revenge on the world by being a success, then I would become a killer myself, and take revenge in the same way that the killers had taken theirs on us. I wanted revenge for my dad who I couldn't ever see or talk to again because of them. I wanted revenge for the suffering of my mother and brother and sisters. I wanted revenge for my own stolen childhood. I wanted revenge for the hunger I was forced to live with and for the fact that I had been born to be a "cockroach".

In order to be able to enact that revenge I decided I would become a soldier because I didn't need a formal education for that, and then I would be able to kill people in the course of war. If I joined the army they would train me in how to shoot and kill effectively and, if I chose, I could then take those skills and use them to fight my own battles, killing people who I had seen doing the same themselves during the genocide and who were now being allowed to go back to their previous lives as if nothing had happened while my family continued to suffer.

It was my belief that if I worked hard enough at whatever military training I could get, then I would become as strong as a superman and I would never have to be a victim again, would never again be hunted through the undergrowth like an animal. I remembered how powerful the soldiers had seemed when they arrived in our village compared to the ragged, barefoot men I was used to, the ones who had seemed so powerful themselves when they took up their machetes and hacked my friends and family to pieces.

I found out where my soldier friends had been moved to and I went to see them, telling them of my ambitions to become a soldier myself, so that I could be like them.

"Why do you want to do that?" they wanted to know.

I couldn't answer that I wanted to be a killer, so I said nothing.

"You are only fifteen," they said, "so you can't join the Rwandan army yet."

As I walked home, feeling even more frustrated. I knew I couldn't spend the next three years starving half to death and talking to my dead father all day long, so I decided that if I couldn't get into the national army I would go to the Congo and join one of the militias as a child soldier. So now I just had to plan how I would do that.

13

THE CONGOLESE DOCTOR

The date for the start of the new school term came and went and I felt deep despair in the following weeks when every day seemed to drag on for ever. I went back almost daily to continue my conversations with my father. One day, when evening was approaching and it came time to go home, I emerged from the bush to find a man walking past. I could tell he was Congolese and I guessed he was a doctor from the nearby hospital. He looked at me warily, unsure if I was going to attack him, beg or steal from him.

"Bonsoir," I said, and he was obviously surprised to be addressed in French by a hungry-looking local kid in a dirty t-shirt, school trousers and flip-flops.

I have always liked getting into conversations with older people and I was happy to answer all his questions as he tried to work out what I was doing there, alone in the bush. He told me his name was Kalombo Thierry.

"Why aren't you in school?" he asked eventually.

"We don't have the money for me to get there," I replied.

"What do you mean?"

"It is a long bus ride away and my family don't have enough money for the fare."

"How much do you need?"

"If I walk for four hours first, then I can get a bus from the town and it will cost me three pounds and twenty pence."

"Do you have all the papers with your grades and reports?"

"Yes."

"I live over there," he pointed to some houses beside the hospital. "Would you bring them to me tomorrow evening, after I finish work?"

Something in his face told me that he liked me and that I had nothing to lose by pursuing the friendship. So, the following evening I took my school papers to his house as he asked. It seemed like paradise to me as he welcomed me in. It was so clean and the floor was actually carpeted. He had a bible and a music system with giant speakers, which we listened to together as we talked and he looked at my papers. Then he gave me seven pounds, the price of a return bus ticket. I couldn't believe that it was actually happening.

"Go to school," he said, "and when you get back come and see me again and let me know how you have got on."

Although I now had an opportunity to move forward, I did not let go of the idea of becoming a killer now that it had taken root in my brain, particularly as I still did not want to spend my life as a primary school teacher. I said nothing about my ambition to the kind doctor, knowing that he would not have approved and would not have wanted to help me if he had known the truth about what was in my heart. Although I was grateful to him for his kindness, I felt a deep resentment that I was forced to rely on charity like this simply in order to get to school. I felt angry at the world that I had been made to worry for so long. Now I decided to go to school until I was eighteen, become as educated as possible, and then I would join the army and enact my plan for revenge.

Because the family were in such a terrible state of hunger I gave two and a half pounds to my mother and used the rest of the money to buy a ticket which would take me all the way from the main road closest to our village, so that I didn't have to walk for four hours on my own with all my luggage. I told myself that I would worry about how to get a ticket home at the end of term when the time came. It felt like a great self-indulgence.

By the time I arrived at the school, however, I was almost two months late for the start of my first term.

"How dare you come this late?" the school manager demanded when I presented myself at the office. "We are almost into the exams already. Your place has been given to another student. It is in the rules. It was announced on the radio that anyone who didn't show up at their school would lose their place within a week. If you want to come here then you have to go to Kigali and get the right paperwork."

I felt like he had punched me in the face because I had now spent all the money the doctor had given me and had nothing to buy a bus ticket to Kigali with. I didn't even have any money to get back home. I was stranded in a strange town, many hours from the village, knowing no-one and having no way of contacting anyone I did know.

"Please," I begged, "give me a chance. I will do my best to catch up."

"No." He was immoveable. To him I was just one more boy amongst hundreds, but to me it seemed liked yet another example of how unfair my life was.

There was another woman in the room. She seemed to be listening to the argument and then she got up and walked out. I argued for a bit longer, unable to stop my voice from cracking as my throat constricted, nor the tears from brimming into my eyes. Finally I was ejected from the office with nothing but the phone number of the Ministry of Education in Kigali, having no idea where I would go now or what I would do, entirely alone.

He had told me where I would find a public telephone in the school, but I had never used a telephone before in my life. I had no idea what I was going to say to them even if I managed to work out how to get through. It was unarguable that I had not got to the school when I was supposed to and so it was fair that I should forfeit my place, even if it didn't seem so to me.

"Okay," I thought to myself, "this is just one more sign that I should find my way to the Congo and become a child soldier. It is obvious that I am never going to be allowed to get an education – and now the school manager will be on my hit list as well."

The woman from the office was waiting for me outside. "Hi," she said and even in my distressed state I noticed that she was beautiful. "My name is Domitienne. I am the Discipline Master here."

I didn't really care. To me she was another member of the team that had just rejected me.

"Let me help you," she said gently, realising how upset I was. "First let's find someone who will look after your bag."

She called over some passing students and asked them to look after my stuff. "Now come back to my house and get a good night's sleep and we will work out what you need to do tomorrow."

Her house, which she shared with another lady who seemed to be her housekeeper, was on the road just outside the school fence. She took me back there, fed me and gave me a bed for the night. It was a very comfortable house with nice towels and a proper bed, very different to home. Despite my exhaustion and the comfort of the bed I only slept fitfully, my brain racing as I tried to plan how I would get to the Congo from there and how I would find someone to train me to be a killer.

The next morning we went to make the call to Kigali, and only then did I realise that it cost money to use a public phone. I must have looked like I was panicking because Domitienne gently took the phone from me, put some money in, dialled the number and then passed me the receiver. When a voice answered I started to talk but there was so much happening in my brain the words wouldn't come out in the right order and I just started crying again, so they hung up on me, wasting my new friend's money.

"Okay," she said, getting out some more coins. "Try again."

This time I managed to hold back the tears when I was connected and I succeeded in explaining my predicament. They asked which school it was that I was trying to get into and when I told them they told me they were coming there on an official visit in a week's time.

"If you wait there for us," they said, "we will see if we can help you."

As I hung up the tears came again. How could I wait a week? Where would I go? I had to find out how to get to the Congo quickly.

"Don't worry," Domitienne said. "I will ask the students to bring your bag to the house and you can stay with me like you were my own child."

Later, once I had calmed down and we were talking about other things, I asked her how I would get to Congo from there.

"Why would you want to get to Congo?" she asked, obviously surprised by the request.

"I just wondered," I tried to sound casual, "because the border is close to where I live."

"Well," she said, looking a little sceptical, "you would need to get a boat across the lake, but it costs a lot of money."

I never had any trouble striking up conversations with adults so during the following week I hung around the school buildings and made a point of meeting and talking to as many of the Congolese teachers as I could find. There was one in particular who was intrigued by how good my French was. Domitienne also gave me permission to come into the school to play basketball with the students, to give me a chance to make some friends.

There were some soldiers camped on a hill above the school, so I went and introduced myself to them as well, telling them a bit of my story and how I and my family had been saved by their colleagues.

After a week, the education officials never arrived from Kigali and the Congolese teacher I had befriended gave me the money to make another call. Domitienne came with me again.

"Okay," the person on the other end of the line said when I had explained my problem again, "we will call your school."

The call came and I have no idea what was said, but without any further delay I was given everything I needed and told to start going to classes. It was a big relief but it didn't change my mind about anything. I was still planning to find a way to get to Congo as soon as I could. The other students were amazing, helping me to catch up with the two months' worth of work with their notes. I couldn't understand why they were being so nice. Some of them had seen me on the basketball court during the previous week and told me how impressed they were with my skills. I was beginning to feel good about myself again for the first time in many months. Maths I still didn't get, but in everything else I was soon catching up.

Domitienne paid for my ticket back to the village at the end of term and I took all my grades to show the Congolese doctor, who agreed to pay for my bus tickets for the rest of my schooling.

Everything that I needed at the school was paid for by the Survivors' Fund. Sometimes, if the holidays were only short, I would not make the trip all the way home and would stay with Domitienne, taking the opportunity to strengthen my friendship with the Congolese teacher.

14

THE GACACA COURTS

I missed the endless views of Lake Kivu that I had enjoyed so much at my last school, but the area around this school was more like a town, with shops and bars, so it felt like I was moving on from my rural background, one step at a time, towards the modern, outside world. My course included chemistry, biology, maths and all the other subjects I would need if I was going to teach in a primary school.

Our school had not had a good basketball team for a long time, but just after I joined the team we beat a rival school for the first time in years, which meant that a lot of the glory reflected onto me and helped boost my popularity and made me a well-known face in the school. I was around a lot when other students had gone home for holidays, talking to whichever members of staff were still there, so many of them came to know me personally. I also grew my hair very long at the time, which probably helped to make me memorable.

By the time I was in the second year at the school my friendship with the Congolese teacher had become even deeper and all the time it was at the back of my mind that he might be able to help me get to Congo to pursue my dream of becoming a killer. He had found out that I loved the theatre and that I was working on the play that I had started in my primary school, gradually putting in more bits about my history and my thoughts on what had happened to me as they had developed over the years and my perspective changed.

"Why don't we put your play on here?" he suggested.

I jumped at the chance, remembering how much I had enjoyed performing in front of an audience before. The teacher worked on it with me and when it was ready we announced a performance date. People from the village that surrounded the school buildings came, along with students, and everyone was encouraged to ask questions afterwards. It was quite a shocking concept in a culture where no one really wanted to talk about the past but, just like before, it worked and the audience opened up to it. I became quite famous in the area for being the man who was writing plays, as well as being known for my sporting skills, reassuring me that I was not a cockroach, that I was a worthwhile person.

"I have a play that you would be really good in," my teacher told me one day.

The play was long and in French and I loved it. I liked the fact that it meant I could improve my French further and also that I could imprint myself deeper on the minds of the other students and teachers, a process that had already started on the basketball court and with my own play.

I was on the verge of asking my Congolese teacher, who was now my friend, if he could help me get to Congo when I was introduced to sociology by a teacher who explained that it was the study of the interactions of people. That sounded very interesting. If I could learn how people interact with one another I would be an even better killer because I would be able to work out where people were and what they would be doing at any particular time of the day or night.

I was becoming a leader of the school in the arts as well as the sports, having such a good time that I decided to put off going to Congo until after I had finished school. The sociology lessons started and we learnt about interactions and about the transformation of people's behaviours and how they are influenced by what they learn and by their environment. We added psychology to the lessons and I started to get good grades and to come out top of the class. I constantly bombarded the teachers with questions.

"So, the people who killed others in the genocide, did they do it because they were born hating people? How did that hatred develop from their life experiences?"

That was when I really started to learn about the political history of Rwanda rather than relying on the gossip of people who had already been indoctrinated by one side or the other.

Not all the students in the class thought that it was good to ask so many questions. Some of them had parents who'd had to leave the country because they had been convicted killers, others were survivors who had suffered and lost even more than me. There were others in the class, however, who were as fascinated by the subject as I was. I decided then that sociology was what I wanted to concentrate on for the rest of my life, trying to contribute to discovering and explaining how some people come to do such bad things.

My mother was told that my father's killers, some of whom we had known as neighbours, had gone back to the scene after I left and cut off his nose so they could show other people in the village just how long and thin the noses of the Tutsis were. Yet when the information was raised in the Gacaca courts, no one pleaded guilty. I can believe that is true because I saw killers taking the hearts, sexual organs and heads of their victims and proudly parading them as trophies of war. In some cases we heard that they even cooked the hearts afterwards in order to celebrate their success, like hunters returning from the bush with a prize antelope. When so many terrible things are happening it is sometimes hard to work out what is real and what is myth or propaganda.

"So the people who were killing us," I said to the teacher one day when we were talking outside class, "were not born bad people? They were taught to hate?"

I suddenly realised that it was not the clubs and the machetes which were killing people, so much as the hatred which caused people to believe they should pick up the weapons in the first place and then use them in service to that hatred. Now that I was coming to understand better what had led up to the genocide against the Tutsi, I had to decide whether I still wanted to go to Congo, or to the army, in order to learn how to hate and kill. I thought about the soldiers who I had admired so much in the village, who had been first my heroes and then my friends, and I realised that I had never seen any of them killing anyone, I had only seen them working to stop other people from killing. It was at this moment that I made the most important choice of my life. I chose to forgive.

This was a time when the local authorities were holding Gacaca courts all round the country. The Gacaca court is a traditional Rwandan system of community justice. Loosely translated it means "justice amongst the grass". Gacaca courts were being used to handle many of the genocide cases at a local level, after the culprits had served some time in prison and were asking to come back to their communities. The idea was to ascertain as many facts as possible about what had happened and who had killed who. There was a lot of information to be gathered because so many of the killings were done in front of witnesses. It was never going to be possible for every death to be investigated and every killer to be tried for every death, there were simply too many for that. The best that could be achieved was a sense within the communities that justice had been served.

During the heat of the genocide the killers were actually proud of what they were doing and wanted people to see. They boasted openly about their terrible deeds. The more people they killed, the more "manly" they felt they were proving themselves to be. For many it was a question of competitiveness, like a war game you might play on a computer where the headcount is just the way of keeping score.

Their mission, they proudly declared, was to eradicate us so completely that their children would "have to ask what a Tutsi was because they would never get to meet one themselves", which was why they felt they should kill children and babies and even unborn foetuses. They convinced themselves that when they were killing they were simply "going to work", even if that work meant dashing newborn babies' heads against the wall or cutting foetuses from their mothers' bellies. Many of the killings, of course, went unpunished simply through lack of evidence. My family, for instance, have never found out who it was that I heard killing my father that day because the deed was done in the bush, not in front of witnesses.

The Gacaca courts were a good system for being seen to dispense justice, but there were always going to be people who would find ways to avoid it. Some of the most powerful people, even those who were already in prison, would pay people not to give evidence against them, thereby ensuring that some stories never got told. It is not hard to buy people's silence when they are poor and hungry. The government also produced lists of killers who had managed to escape to other countries in Africa and Europe without ever being tried for their crimes at all.

I asked if I could attend some of these courts in order to better understand what had happened and how reconciliation between the two sides might work. When I got there I saw people asking for forgiveness, admitting in front of a crowd the terrible things they had done. As would often happen, some of them claimed it wasn't their fault because they were drunk at the time and did not know what they were doing. It was true that many of them used to drink large quantities of beer to pluck up their courage before "going to work", but they would also drink more afterwards to celebrate the success of their missions – or perhaps to numb the pain of their guilty consciences. Many admitted that at the time they were proud of their achievements. I heard one man in our village telling of how he returned home after killing many people in the church and had boasted that he deserved to eat a whole goat by himself because he had done so well.

I decided I would also go back to my village to see if the killers there would be willing to apologise to my family and ask for forgiveness for what they had done to us.

The next time I got home I found a Gacaca court already underway with a man who had been brought to the village from the prison where he was serving his sentence. I stood at the back, listening as the man described the sins he had committed, and I realised he was talking about the night when my brother my mother and I had seen so many people hacked down by the light of the blazing bonfire.

"I'm really sorry," he was saying, "to all the families and the people who had to see me doing this."

It made me think again about my plan to become a killer. I looked around at my childhood friends in the crowd, most of whom were Hutus, people who I had gone into the forest with when we were young, looking after cows and goats together. Was I really going to come back and kill them all? Or was I going to be strong enough to do the bigger thing and forgive them? If I forgave them then there was a possibility that the hatred that had cascaded down the generations could be ended. If I decided to kill them instead, I would simply be continuing the destructive line of hatred and vengeance, and it would never end. The only way to break the cycle was by deciding to do so.

Protais felt the same and we organised a genocide commemoration event, inviting as many members of the family as we knew who were still alive, and everyone else in the village. We went to houses of different people, including the ones who were coming out of prison having finished their sentences for the genocide crimes they had committed, inviting them to a remembrance walk and a visit to the memorial at Mibirizi Church.

"We are not going to ask you to give any testimony or anything like that," we assured everyone, "unless you feel there is something you want to say. We would just like you to be with us."

After the service at the memorial we went home for what we call a "washing of the hands" with food and drink for guests, where survivors and leaders gave testimonies. Some perpetrators also stood up and spoke of some of the killings that happened in Gasharu. They confessed their part in it and all hoped that the young children were learning lessons from the mistakes that they had made.

We then hugged each other as a sign of forgiveness and reconciliation. After that it became easier to meet and greet those men in the street, although there are still people who cannot forgive and can't bring themselves to shake hands with the past killers. There are also some killers who still believe that they were right in what they did and openly admit that they would do the same again if they are ever given the chance, and there are others who deny the genocide against the Tutsi ever happened. Scholars describe this as one of the stages of the act of genocide.

I know reconciliation is not something that can happen in one day. It is a process and different people get to the end at different times, and I understand that there will always be sorrow for the people who went through those experiences. But if we continue to fear and avoid those who committed the killings, then they will become isolated from their communities and reconciliation will be delayed still longer.

15

FALLING IN LOVE

In 2006, two young Belgian girls came to the school for a few months to do internships and to give us an introduction to ICT (Information and Communications Technology). I was eighteen by then and they were just a year older than me. With their guidance we started to learn what computers are and how to use them.

Since it was only a few years since I'd seen my first television set, this was a significant jump up the learning curve. The machines seemed such alien things that to start with I was scared to even enter the laboratory where they were set up, fearful that they might be able to read my mind. I was a grown man who was supposed to be training to teach children and I was scared of the magical powers of computers – scared but also intrigued.

One of the girls was a beautiful blond called Olivia. A lot of our teachers, including the headmaster, liked the girls and tried to date them. Most of them preferred Olivia because her friend smoked cigarettes, and most people in Rwanda don't like that. A woman who smokes in Rwanda is always judged very harshly.

Our first task was to master the keyboard as a tool for writing, just like the pen or pencil. As I started to learn how to type, very slowly, and began to write things, I wrote about the genocide, the subject which always filled my mind and my soul. Olivia noticed and started asking me questions about my past and about what had happened during those months. It felt good to have someone showing an interest in the stories and the feelings that I had stored up in my head, although it was often difficult to talk about them without becoming emotional.

She started to show up at the basketball court to watch the games and I realised that she liked me as much as I liked her. It was an exciting realisation, made all the more exciting by the fact that we had to be discreet about our growing feelings for one another because I didn't want the teachers who liked her to find out.

We started to date but I was really naïve about everything to do with girls and how things should be done. My only experiences were watching the formal courtships of my sisters with their boyfriends, when I was very little, and a few alarming glimpses of porn. I didn't even know how to kiss. The closest I came to being romantic was taking a flower to give to her each time she invited me to the house where they were staying, outside the school gates. I also wrote her a short poem in French. My visits to her house had to be done in secret because I would have been punished if I had been caught leaving the school grounds.

The fact that we had fallen in love made it all the more important that I mastered the computers so that I could email her once she had left Rwanda and returned to her life in Belgium. When she first told me that we would be able to do that, I had trouble grasping the whole concept of the internet and how I might be able to get access to it. She took me to a cyber café and showed me how to work the machines. At that stage I could still only type with one finger, laboriously searching out the keys I needed for every letter, and at school it would take me all day just to do a five-hundred-word essay. The extra, practical tuition from Olivia, however, meant that I started to do better, even better than some of the students from Kigali who had previously been more familiar with computers than those of us from distant, rural areas.

The more she showed me the more I began to see the possibilities that technology might provide for introducing myself to people outside Rwanda, getting my voice and my story out to other places, and at the same time for learning more about how the outside world worked. It was like a door had opened, allowing me step out of my past in the village on the other side of the forest and into the rest of the world.

The weeks that Olivia was with us went all too fast and as the day of her departure approached she suggested that we should meet in Kigali so that we could spend some time together before she flew home. I couldn't imagine how I was going to be able to get permission to go to Kigali when all the staff knew my story and knew I did not come from there, that my home was in the opposite direction. I was going to have to make up a complete lie about going home to see my Mum, which made me very uncomfortable. The temptation of this romantic adventure, however, was too much to resist. I can't remember the details of what I told them now, but I managed to get the time out.

The thought of going to the big city for the first time was very daunting and I didn't have the nerve to just turn up there on my own. I had a friend in class, Amani, who used to sit at the same desk as me, who was a city boy and knew his way around Kigali. I persuaded him to come with me and to advise me on what I should do. He was the only person I confided the truth to. He invited me to stay with his family and I accepted because to say no would have seemed rude, but Olivia was expecting me to spend the night with her in the big house where she was staying. Again I was wading into a situation that was way out of my depth, and all the more exciting for that.

The girls had been taken to Kigali in the school car, but since no one was supposed to know where we were going, Amani and I had to find our own way on the bus. Olivia had given me her mobile number but at that stage neither Amani nor I had a phone, but his brother, Henry, did, so he contacted Olivia for us once we had arrived in what seemed to me to be a huge, bustling metropolis. We all met in a café for lunch and Olivia very kindly paid for everything since none of us had any money at all. We didn't worry because we always assumed that white people had enough money for whatever eventuality arose, but looking back now she was probably puzzled as to why I had turned up with two other people.

After lunch she and I held hands as Amani and Henry showed us around the city and we went to watch a basketball match. It was all very cute but I could see people looking at us, wondering how a young black boy like me got to be dating a tall, beautiful white girl, looking so glamorous in her sunglasses. It felt good but at the same time I was nervous about what would happen next. I wanted to be romantic but I had no idea how to go about it. Henry had given me a bit of advice beforehand, like telling me I should give her a kiss, but I was very unsure how to do that and I just couldn't pluck up the courage to try, for fear of getting it all wrong and either scaring her off or making a fool of myself. I could see that she wanted to kiss me as much as I wanted to kiss her, but I was just too Rwandan and too polite to be able to make the necessary first move.

She bought us dinner and then Henry had to leave.

"Let's go back to my room," Olivia suggested.

We went to the house where she and her friend were staying. She turned the television on and went into her bedroom, calling me to follow, leaving Amani sitting in the living room with the television. This was the first time I had ever been in such an intimate situation with a girl and I had no idea what to do next. My whole body was shaking with nerves. She assumed that Amani was still with us because he was just not taking the hint, so I explained that it was actually me who was making things complicated because I needed him to stay if I was going to find my way back to his house later.

"But you can spend the night here with me," she said, as if it was the most obvious thing in the world, and my shaking grew even more intense. I thought that Amani would be angry if I told him that I didn't want to accept his hospitality and stay the night at his house, and then he might give me away to the teachers when we got back. I couldn't work out what would be the correct way to behave towards both of them.

Not surprisingly, Olivia couldn't understand what I was talking about. Why was I being so weird when she was offering me this wonderful opportunity to be with her?

"It's not going to be possible," I said, "let's just have a conversation and then I will come back tomorrow to say goodbye before you fly."

For about an hour we talked and kissed and I did it very badly, but I still felt very pleased with myself for having kissed a girl at all when Amani and I left to go back to his house. I have no idea what was going on in her head.

The next morning when we went back to meet up with the girls before going to catch our bus back to school, Olivia took me back into the bedroom and told me that she loved me. She said she wanted to stay in touch and that she would come back to Rwanda soon. She gave me a very nice Nokia phone which contained all her contact details and I still use that SIM card to this day. Very few people had nice phones in Rwanda at that time, not even the teachers, so it was a hugely generous gesture. I liked the idea that we would still be linked, even after she had flown back to Europe. I knew nothing about how to work it. I didn't even understand that it was set to "vibrate" mode, but I couldn't believe my good fortune. She also gave me forty pounds so that I could buy more call time when I needed it. Once she had gone I felt I had to give half of the money to Amani to thank him for coming all the way to Kigali with me and looking after me, the rest I put on the phone.

All too soon it was time for us to leave and Olivia came with us to the bus station to see us off.

"I'll call you," she said, hugging me as Amani and I got on the bus.

When we got to our seats and I looked out the window I could see she was crying and as the bus drew forward she ran alongside, pressing her hand to the glass.

"Stop the bus!" some of the other passengers shouted at the driver, "This boy has stolen something from that girl!"

The driver slammed on the brakes and told me to get out and talk to her. I could feel everyone's eyes on me as I walked back off. I hugged her and she kissed me on the forehead in full view of everyone, a very un-Rwandan public display of affection which left me simultaneously hot with embarrassment and flushed with pride.

"I love you!" she said.

Looking up I could see the whole bus watching this scene through the windows, realising that they had misunderstood the situation and shocked by what they were seeing. This was not the way Rwandans ever behaved in public.

When I climbed back on to take my seat next to Amani again I had to avoid everyone's eyes, deeply embarrassed to have been part of such an undignified spectacle, but also a little proud of myself at the same time. Throughout the two-and- a-half-hour journey no one said a word to us. It was like everyone was shocked and trying to make sense of what they had just seen.

On the journey the phone vibrated in my pocket, making me jump out of my skin. Amani took it off me and explained that it was just Olivia ringing me from the airport to tell me she loved me and to say goodbye once again.

We kept in touch for a while. She ordered a necklace online and had it sent to me, which was later stolen and which I still miss. She sent me photos and slowly I learnt how easily people could stay in touch with technology. When she sent me emails, telling me how much she loved and missed me, I would buy time in a cyber café so that I could read them and reply, although I think my replies were probably a bit of a disappointment to her as I never seemed to have enough time and had difficulty thinking of the right things to say to her. Mainly it was just me telling her that I loved her too. Looking back now I can see that she would write a whole page and I would only be able to reply with one sentence, totally unromantic and usually pretty bad English.

Eventually her tone changed and she started to say that she didn't think our relationship was going to work after all and then she closed down all the connections we had, which made me very sad. I know she has a boyfriend now, because I was also in contact with her friend and heard through her, so I guess it all became too difficult and perhaps the intensity of her adventure in Africa wore off with time.

16

UNIVERSITY LIFE

The next time I travelled to Kigali was when I spent three weeks teaching maths in a private Belgian school as an intern. Although I did not like maths particularly, it was the easiest subject to teach, especially at primary level, because it is practical and easy to plan for. The system of teaching was very different to anything I had experienced and I didn't enjoy it because I was aware that I was learning more than I was teaching, which was good for me but not so good for the pupils and therefore ultimately unsatisfying. The pupils were from rich families, some of them the children of white diplomats.

Having reached the end of my schooling, now was the time for me to apply to university, once I knew that I had good enough grades to qualify. I chose the National University of Rwanda in Butare and applied to study sociology. I passed the necessary exam but that was only the first hurdle. A much bigger problem, as with the bus fares to get to and from school, was the money. University was not free so I was going to need a Survivors' Fund scholarship to pay the fees, but to get one from the primary teaching section was hard.

In 2008 I had a gap year and I spent some time teaching Kinyarwanda, French and geography in a private high school. Most of my pupils were around twelve years old, only five or six years younger than me, and the best bit of the job was having conversations with them about their lives and about my life and how I had succeeded in getting an education even though I had come from a penniless rural family.

Like most teachers, the moments in my life that have made me happiest are the ones when a young person has told me that I have inspired them or made a difference to their lives, giving them hope or showing them the way forward. There is no feeling as good as that for me.

That was also the year when the Rwandan government decided to change the official language of the country from French to English due to the decision to become part of the Commonwealth and to alleged diplomatic difficulties with France, following their handling of the genocide. That meant that I had to improve my English quickly so that I would be ready to study in that language.

I now harboured dreams of becoming a great sociologist and studying abroad, and if I was going to stand any chance of fulfilling them I was going to have to work twice as hard as everyone else. Following my success at school my courage, which had seeped away during the months when I couldn't raise the bus fare, was returning and I remembered my father's dreams that Protais and I would be able to do all the things he was not able to do. I would feel sad to think that Dad wasn't there to see what we were doing, but I would still get the feeling that he was writing me letters from wherever he was, which I could see and read inside my head, just as I had felt when I spent all those days sitting in the bush, on the spot where he died. Now, however, the contents of the letters was changing, encouraging me to keep working and no longer pointing me towards the path of revenge through killing.

Once I got to university I spent every spare hour I had reading or going to classes to improve my English. I used to take books into the forest and read aloud to the trees in order to work on my spoken English. I asked the teachers and professors endless questions because I assumed they knew everything about everything. Sometimes they would even become angry if they didn't know the answers and didn't believe the questions were relevant to sociology, thinking that I was just testing them, but I really just wanted the answers to all the questions that came buzzing into my head, day and night.

Although it was great that the government was making it possible for more people to get access to education than ever before, many of the professors and teachers were not very inspiring. They simply taught what was in the curriculum and the students were then tested on it and expected to memorise the information and regurgitate the same facts back to show that they had learnt them. Very few of the teachers suggested books or articles that I should read to broaden my knowledge base, I had to discover those for myself. Often the teachers didn't even turn up. At one stage, when no one had turned up for a month, I and another student complained to the Rector of the University who then contacted the Dean of the Faculty. All three hundred students in the department were called in and they demanded to know who had complained about them. The problem then became the fact that we had complained, not the fact that we weren't being taught well.

There were some professors who agreed with what we were saying, but they told us we should have gone to the Dean and not over his head to the Rector. But the Dean was one of the teachers who wasn't showing up for classes, so we couldn't have gone to him. Some of our fellow students were also cross with us, saying that we would all now be awarded bad grades because we had upset the staff.

Now I understand that the problem stems from the fact that the teachers are so badly paid they have to take other jobs, which means they can't always get to their classes.

While at university I spent a lot of time in the "American Corner", meeting as many people as I could. If I came across any white people I would try to engage them in conversation, even if they did not speak English, wanting them to correct me if I made mistakes. Another trick was to take books into the forest and read them out loud without necessarily understanding the meaning of the words I was saying. I would also shamelessly ask people if they had any books that they could give to me. If I saw someone reading a book I would ask if I could read it after them. I never wanted to miss a single opportunity to learn something new and as a result I now have a huge collection of books from that period.

I also began to explore the internet further, discovering that through sites like YouTube, I could watch sociology lectures and courses that I could follow in tandem with the university course, and through Twitter and Facebook and Skype I could make contact with anyone in the world I wanted to, without it costing anything. Not all of them would respond to my approaches, of course, but many did. I was discovering the tools needed to talk to the world. It wasn't all plain sailing to start with. The internet signal at the university was not good and would keep buffering, which meant that watching a thirty-minute lecture could take anything up to several hours, but those pauses would give me a chance to think and take notes and were a small price to pay for the intellectual treasure chest that was opening up for me.

Protais was also in university by then, having finished at seminary school and decided that the priesthood was not for him. We were very conscious that we were two of the very few surviving men from our father's family after our last uncle died in 2005, and my brother really wanted to marry and have children one day, which he couldn't have done if he had become a priest.

In 2010, in my second year at university, an American lady called Roberta came to Butare to teach theatre in the university's Arts and Drama department. I befriended her and told her a bit of my story and the reasons why I did theatre in order to share my thoughts and experiences. Having heard what I had to say she sent me an application form which said that the British Council of Switzerland was looking for "passionate young people from post-conflict countries" to talk at a conference. She encouraged me to apply, which I did. Part of the application required me to create a one-minute video about myself. There were also some American film makers, Rob and Lisa, working in the department on a film called "Sweet Dreams", who had got to know me at the American Corner and had been using me as a translator, so I went to them for help with that.

When I heard my application had been accepted to give a five-minute speech in Switzerland, I set about preparing it carefully with the help of my various mentors in the university. I was eager to make the maximum impact with my words.

Up until that point all my experiences of the world outside Rwanda had been gained through talking to foreign visitors like Olivia and the visiting professors, or through the internet. Now I was actually going to be travelling for real. Initially we were flying to Kenya and then we were going to transfer to another plane in order to fly to Berne on Emirates Airline.

This was the first time I had ever been to an airport, let alone boarded a plane. My senses were sent reeling by an onslaught of new and incomprehensible sights, sensations and experiences. I was so confused I wasn't sure that I was going to be able to work out what I was meant to do. Somehow I got through the airport and onto the plane, but then I couldn't understand what the cabin crew were telling us about life jackets and oxygen masks. I had no idea what to expect and was astonished to see people eating meals and drinking like they were sitting in a restaurant in their local street. When I looked out the window and saw the sea below I remembered them talking about life jackets and felt sure this was going to be the end for me.

17

TEARS IN GENEVA

Arriving in Berne I was met and transferred to a train because the conference was taking place in Geneva at the headquarters of the International Red Cross. This was another new experience since we have no railways in Rwanda. It was so big and so clean and so comfortable, but none of the passengers were talking to one another. Everyone was acting as if they didn't know there was anyone else in the carriage. If we had been on a bus in Rwanda everyone would have been talking loudly, asking one another questions, telling jokes or engaging in hot debates about politics or food. Some would be listening to radios, and the driver would have been playing whatever he wanted to listen to over the speakers as well, which might be music or might be a football match. In this train there was just the sound of the tracks passing beneath us and the calm announcements at each station, which neither my English nor my French was not good enough to interpret. Apart from that there was silence. I couldn't understand it. Did they all hate each other? I didn't like it and part of me wanted to go home, although the other part was almost breathless with excitement at so many new experiences.

There were twelve of us who had been brought in to speak, and we were going to be there for ten days, trying to master modern life with all the technology that people in the West grow so used to they don't even think about it, like ordering things online or using a credit card to just "tap and go". Everything was so new and strange and amazing. Everyone looked so busy and was walking so fast. It was also a shock to be so cold. They had told us to bring warm clothes, but the sort of clothes we would have considered warm in Rwanda were useless in Switzerland. I had to borrow some real clothes off one of our hosts just in order to be able to survive outside on the street.

When it came time for me to walk out onto the stage and talk directly about my experiences, without hiding behind a character in a play as I normally did, I only managed to talk for a minute and a half before I was overcome with emotion. My throat tightened and closed and the words refused to come. I was unable to stop myself from crying, and many of the people in the audience cried with me.

The organisers had also made time for us to do some sight-seeing while we were in the country. We were taken on another train to Lausanne and when we got there I went for a walk around the edge of the lake with another boy from the group, who had been flown in from Sudan. We had become good friends, both being so far from home and going through the same experiences. An old man was listening to us as we talked about the things that had surprised us on the trip so far.

"Welcome monkeys," the old man suddenly said. We looked at him in surprise and he laughed. "Yeah, welcome."

I was offended but I had no idea how to react. So I just said, "thank you".

Afterwards I remembered that I had been told that at football matches in Europe the white people in the crowd would shout these sorts of things at the black players on the pitch and it suddenly made me feel angry. For so many years I had been told that I was a cockroach and a second-class citizen. I had thought that those times were behind me and that I had proved myself to be just the same as anyone else, but now I was reminded that many white people thought I was inferior because of the colour of my skin. It was a shock and a disappointment.

While I was there I befriended the family of the Director of the British Council and when I told them my story they said they wanted to help me. They suggested they should sponsor me and with that money I bought my first computer, a Toshiba laptop, which I used to learn to type properly and to fully explore the possibilities of technology and the internet. It was another enormous leap forward into the modern world – no more expensive visits to cyber cafés in Butare or Kigali.

It is my experience that whenever anyone hears my story they are always moved and shocked and often want to find ways to help in the efforts to fight hate. After my extremely short talk in Geneva an older Swiss man called Jean Cordey came up to hug me and said that he really wanted to help in some way, although he didn't know how, and asked me to stay in touch. I always like to keep in touch with people because you never know what opportunities a friendship will lead to. Jean Cordey worked with an organisation called Geneva World, which encouraged young people all over the world to use art to express what things meant to them. We exchanged emails and I told him that I was thinking a lot about the concept of reconciliation, and about the killers who were now coming out of prison and returning to the communities where they had enacted the genocide, living once more as neighbours to the survivors. The most important thing seemed to be that both sides should learn how to forgive whatever had happened in the past, get over any feelings of hatred and work together to create a better future for all the children of Rwanda, whatever their family histories might be. Because I was thinking about the situation so much I kept coming up with new ideas. One of them was that the prisoners should be taught some meditation techniques before they were released. I had never meditated myself but I had read a lot about the subject and it seemed like it might help them become both more self aware and more aware of other people's emotional needs.

My American professor always told me that if I ever had an idea I should write it down. So I created a very basic concept paper and sent it to Jean Cordey, my friend in Geneva. He liked the idea and said he would like to be involved in making it a reality. He refined the proposal and took it to the former CEO of Red Cross International and to the managers at Geneva University's Hospitals. He told me that the director there also liked the idea. He wrote to tell me that things were "looking promising". He prepared a budget and job descriptions; the funding proposals were accepted and the project was due to start in September 2012. At that moment there were international news reports that Rwanda was supporting the militia group, M23, who were fighting a war in Congo and so all international funding schemes were put on hold and Jean Cordey told me that the Swiss government advised their nationals not to travel to Rwanda and the region. Something way beyond my control, or the control of any individuals, had impacted our lives again, stopping the project in its tracks. It was a sobering reminder that all of us are vulnerable to the repercussions of other people's actions, even when they don't directly involve us.

Jean Cordey felt terrible that everything had ground to a halt and worried that he had let me down. I assured him it wasn't his fault any more than it was mine. He then sent me a story he had written which was a metaphor for someone taking their own life. He told me he was thinking of writing his autobiography and I encouraged him because from the things he had already told me I could tell he had had an interesting life, a life that I was certainly happy to read about. He sent a draft of the manuscript to me and my friend, Hassan Bizimana, who I was planning to have work on the project with me, asking for my comments. The story told of how he was abused as a child and rejected by his mother and also talked about how disappointed he was that our project had failed and how he blamed himself. We emailed back and forth until one day he fell silent and I heard nothing else from him.

Unable to get an answer to any of my emails I kept searching online for news of Jean Cordey but there was nothing for more than a year, then one day I stumbled across a message talking about how he had taken his own life. When I checked the dates I realised that it had happened a few days after he sent me his autobiography. You never know what is going on in the minds of those you meet. If someone from one of the safest, most peaceful and most prosperous countries in the world could be driven to such depths of despair by the way the world treated them, it was no wonder that I was still unable to talk to an audience about my childhood experiences without the tears overwhelming and silencing me.

When I got back to Butare from Switzerland the video makers introduced me to some Americans who were looking for someone who could teach them the Kinyarwanda language. I enjoy teaching and I enjoy getting to know new people from other countries, so I accepted the job.

When they came to the end of their time in Butare they threw a Christmas party and I was one of the people they invited to attend the party that took place at their new place in Kigali. Another was a British Red Cross worker called Tejas Barot and we got talking. He showed a lot of interest in my life and we exchanged stories long into the evening. He was working in the prisons so he knew a lot about the Rwandan situation and about the problem of the killers who were now being introduced back into the communities where they had committed their atrocities. After the party we kept in touch on Facebook. I felt we had a lot in common but I had no idea what an important part he would play in my life a little later.

Finding enough money to support ourselves as students was always a problem, particularly if you had no job and no wealthy family. The government gave us just £25 a month to meet all our expenses, which was hard to survive on, even in a country as cheap as Rwanda, and I was always looking for other ways to make a bit of extra spending money or to save on my living costs. Soon after arriving I became very friendly with another student called Patrick and discovered that he was working as a Discipline Master in a Catholic School, Indatwa n'Inkesha, at the same time as taking the sociology course. That meant that he often couldn't get to the lectures. So I agreed to attend on his behalf, passing on everything as I learnt it. That involved us spending a great deal of time together and I became very friendly with his family, who supported me a lot and treated me like I was also their son. In the end Patrick became my best friend. He was a great student and was very successful in his exams and I also benefited from the arrangement because nothing cements a subject in your brain more firmly than having to teach it to someone else. We were both doing very well and for the first time in my life I began to believe that perhaps I could be hopeful for the future despite all the setbacks; perhaps I could exercise some control over my own future, perhaps things really could change, even for a boy from a background like mine.

I remained at university for four years and the roads of Butare got to know my feet well. It is a small town, dominated by the university and the student population, so there are plenty of bars and clubs and everyone knows one another. When people look back now they talk about that time as being a golden era for the university, a period when the standards of education were high and the teachers were good, despite our complaints at the time.

At the same time as studying sociology I continued to write plays and attend drama workshops. I also became a volunteer journalist on Salus, the university radio station which was sponsored by UNICEF. The fact that I was presenting shows meant that I became well known around town and made a lot of friends. I started by doing a half-hour comedy show each week, after Ben, one of my friends from the university theatre troop, who was also a journalist, asked if I would like to do a regular comedy broadcast with him.

I enjoyed it for a while but as I progressed further with my sociology studies I realised that a large part of any comedian's repertoire relies on sexist and racist observations, so I decided that I couldn't really continue along those lines. I started doing news reporting instead, especially following-up the stories of other survivors who had been through similar experiences to me. Then I moved on to telling the stories of musicians and artists, both Rwandan and international, and doing talk shows.

For my dissertation I wanted to write about people who had endured a different life to the majority. There is an island, Iwawa, in the middle of Lake Kivu, which lies between Congo and Rwanda. On it is a government centre for the rehabilitation of young drug addicts. The men stay there for a year and learn vocational skills like bricklaying, carpentry and tailoring, as well as basic hygiene and self discipline. Some Western media had described it as a prison. It became a controversial subject and even the President talked about an article which had appeared in the *New York Times* by a journalist who compared the island to Alcatraz. I couldn't imagine what such a place would be like. I wanted to go and see for myself from a sociological point of view, rather than political or journalistic.

When I pitched the idea to my American professor, Dr Simeon Wiehler, he loved it and encouraged me to go ahead. My classmates, on the other hand, couldn't understand why I wanted to complicate my life for nothing. Most people didn't believe that I would ever get permission to even land on such a controversial place, let alone stay there, asking questions.

Undaunted, and determined to prove all the doubters wrong, I packed a bag with potatoes and rice, enough food to survive, and all my papers and boarded a boat to the island.

Not only did the guards allow me onto the island, they also allowed me to talk to the inmates, spending the day with them and recording their stories, many of which were very shocking, even after everything that I had experienced as a child. There was one young man who told me how he had raped his own grandmother while on drugs. Another told me how he had travelled to Uganda where the dealers had hired a surgeon to open up his body and insert a package of drugs. When he returned to Rwanda they cut him open again and took the drugs out.

"How much were you paid for that?" I asked.

"About ten dollars," he shrugged.

In this world people have to do whatever they can just to survive.

18

MEETING THE PROFESSOR

I was still spending a huge amount of time on the internet, searching out extra educational opportunities. One of the lectures that I watched on YouTube was on the subject of multiculturalism and interculturalism and was given by Professor Tariq Modood. The Professor had a lot of interesting things to say, so I went further by researching the words "multiculturalism" and "interculturalism" on Google. I was hooked.

There was something about the professor's delivery that I liked. He spoke clearly, using simple words that I could hear and understand without any difficulty. I looked for more of his lectures on YouTube and then I wrote to him to tell him that I liked his work but was not completely sure that it fitted in our situation in Rwanda.

He replied, agreeing that it probably didn't fit, but then he started to send me papers that he was working on so that I could study the subject more thoroughly. He didn't have to do that, he simply wanted to help me come to some sort of understanding. The first one was on the subject of Islamophobia.

The American Professor, Dr Simeon Wiehler, who was visiting the university in Butare at the time, was teaching us critical sociology. I was able to ask him a great many follow-up questions about the things that I was learning and he became my mentor, helping me to find the answers I needed on the internet. He became so deeply entrenched in our culture that he eventually married a Rwandan woman.

"I think Professor Modood is very interesting," I told him, "but he is based at Bristol University in England so how can I get to learn from him?"

"You have said you want to travel and study abroad," he pointed out, "you need to approach him and ask him for what you want."

"Would you write to him for me?" I asked, thinking that it might help my credibility if an international professor spoke up for me.

"You need to do that for yourself," he said. "I can't do it for you."

I thought about it and realised that he was right. Despite starting in a poor, rural village and enduring genocide, I had still got myself to university and had achieved the highest grades in my department. I should be confident enough of my abilities to do this for myself. I realised it would look better if I took the initiative and approached the professor directly with my request. It would show that I had drive and initiative.

People like Dr Wiehler, who showed confidence in me and showed me that I was good enough to achieve the things I dreamed about, have been the ones who have given me the greatest gifts in my life.

So what, I wondered, did I need to do in order to apply for a place at a British university? I read online that I needed to prepare a "personal statement". I didn't know what that was so I did more research, then wrote something which included the material I had sent to the British Council when applying to do the talk in Switzerland, and then asked Dr Wiehler to proofread it for me. I also had to take an English test. I had to pay for it, but my sponsors in Switzerland kindly agreed to help with that. So many people were helping me when I asked. It was like I was creating a supportive village for myself with all the people I was finding and connecting to.

I told Professor Modood that I was going to apply and he was very encouraging in his emails, although I got the feeling that he didn't want to build my hopes up too far. I guess someone like him hears from a lot of hopefuls and knows that the odds are always stacked against success, simply due to there being too many people for too few places.

Bristol University replied to my application. They offered me a place, but with no offer of funding. My heart sank. If I couldn't find the money for a four-pound bus ticket to get to school, what hope did I have of financing myself to fly to England, pay for a course and support myself for a year?

The idea of being unable to take the next step simply because I was poor, as had happened before with the bus fare, was unthinkable. Just as I had found the kind Congolese doctor in my hour of need, I had to believe there was going to be an answer to this problem too.

First I decided to try my luck at some other universities. I wrote to other professors in international universities in the Netherlands, the US and Canada but none of them even wrote back to me. At the same time I wrote back to Professor Modood, asking him how I could get funding. He didn't have any suggestions beyond asking around in Rwanda. I wrote to all the official bodies in the country who might have been able to help, but I couldn't find anyone.

One day, at genocide commemoration time, I was talking on Facebook with Tejas, my friend from the Red Cross, who I had met at the party. He asked how I was doing and I told him all about wanting to go to Bristol to do a master's degree with a professor there who I really admired. I hadn't realised at that stage that Tejas was a British citizen. He was obviously surprised that I had been offered a place at such a prestigious university.

"Who was the professor you were in touch with?" Tejas asked.

"Professor Tariq Modood."

"That's amazing," Tejas laughed. "He's a good friend and a former colleague of my Dad's. They have published some papers together and we are family friends. He's a great guy. He makes things happen. Send me the documents and I will talk to him."

Unable to believe the coincidence, I sent the documents, although I couldn't imagine anything would come of it. A few days later I received an email from the professor informing me that he had spoken to Tejas, who had sung my praises, and had consequently asked the university authorities to waive my tuition fee. If the university agreed to that, he went on, then he would like to invite me to stay with him and his wife, Glynthea, in their house for the duration of the course, free of charge. I hardly dared to breathe as I waited to hear how the university authorities would react to such a request.

The professor's recommendation obviously carried considerable weight because the university did agree to waive my fee as he had requested, but I still needed to find at least £8,600 so that I could live during the year I would be spending in Bristol. That was almost nine million Rwandan Francs, and from my short experience of Switzerland I knew exactly how expensive European countries could be for students. I also had to have at least that much money in my bank account for a month before I would be able to get a visa.

I now had only two months left to find the rest of the money before the start of the course. Despite all these lucky breaks it seemed like that was as close as I was going to get to Bristol. Yet again I was going to be unable to take advantage of the opportunities being offered to me because of being poor. I told Tejas my problem.

"Okay," he said. "I will lend you the money. I will put it into your account and leave it there for a month so the authorities can see it. Then you can repay me once you have your visa."

It was an incredibly trusting gesture from a friend and got me over the next hurdle, although I still needed money on which to live. I explained the problem to Professor Modood, who told others at the university my story, asking them to help raise the necessary money. An endowment fund set up to assist international students, anonymously offered to provide £10,000 for my living expenses. It was another giant leap forward and I felt hopeful once more that I might just be going to succeed in my dream.

I also had to pay £3,000 for pre-sessional English courses but the language centre agreed to waive those fees too, probably thanks to Professor Modood's efforts yet again. It was, however, crucial that I passed these English courses otherwise I would be sent straight back to Rwanda. There would be no point wasting everyone's time by sitting through a course if I couldn't speak the language well enough to benefit from it.

I also needed to find some more money to buy the plane ticket to the UK and whatever clothes I needed to take with me for the following year, plus the necessary bus fares for travelling around Rwanda saying goodbye to all my friends and family.

While at Butare I had been involved in an arts and healthcare programme and while attending a forum on Arts in Healthcare in Kigali I had met Professor Jill Sonke from a university in Florida. We were using theatre to assess the problems that Rwandan families were facing like family planning and the spread of HIV/AIDs. I had told her all about being accepted by Bristol University, which she thought was a great story.

"I still need to raise a bit more money for my ticket and the things I need to pay for before I leave."

"How much do you need?" she asked.

"I think about a thousand pounds."

"Ok", she said, "I'll do a crowdfunding scheme to raise the money."

That was the first time I had heard about crowdfunding. She was true to her word and within a week I had about four thousand dollars, donated by people from all over the world.

The process of raising the money to travel and study in England had taught me many things. It had taught me that you will never get anything unless you ask for it and that you must never give up trying, no matter how many obstacles are placed in your path.

More than anything, however, it taught me that there are many good, kind and generous people in the world, who will reach out a hand to help you if they believe you are doing the right thing. Each one of them had helped me to shake off the niggling fears that had always been at the back of my mind, that I actually was no more than a cockroach in the world.

19

A MASTER'S AT BRISTOL

When I arrived in Bristol there was no one to meet me off the plane, but I had enough money to get a bus from the airport to the centre of town. Bristol is an ancient city in the south-west of England which boasts two major universities and a number of other colleges of further education. I liked the fact that the roads were so smooth and free of potholes, the buses so nice and clean, but still no one talked to anyone else during the journey, all of them reading books or phones or tablets, most with earphones isolating them even further from their fellow travellers.

There are about six times as many people living in the city as in Butare, and a great many more roads and roaring streams of traffic to navigate. I felt a very long way from home as I descended from the bus and tried to work out which direction I should walk in next, hauling my luggage along with me.

I had a map, but I'm terrible at map reading so I had to ask people for help at every corner. They were all as helpful as they could be but I still felt very lost, wondering how I would manage for more than a year if I couldn't even read a map and was so hopeless at interacting with the machinery of modern life.

It was August and the professor and his wife were still on their summer holidays, but the university had agreed to let me lodge for free in a hostel until they returned.

As in Switzerland, everyone on the streets was in such a hurry, all avoiding eye contact with one another, and I felt very lonely. One of the biggest shocks was finding that the sun didn't always set at six in the evening, that sometimes in the summer it could still be light at nine or even later. How much easier our lives would have been in the village if we hadn't spent half of every day in darkness.

Everything about the university was so new and clean and efficient. The internet was incredibly fast and there was so much gleaming glass everywhere. The rooms were very different to my classrooms in Rwanda. It was more like being in someone's living room than a classroom, with nice comfortable chairs and no broken windows or noisy air conditioners. You had to swipe a plastic card to unlock the doors, like in a modern hotel, so it felt very safe.

When I wrote home to friends, describing the classrooms and telling them that there were girls sitting around in shorts and mini skirts they couldn't believe it.

"Man," one of them wrote back, "you are not in a classroom. You are sitting in a club!"

When Professor Modood and his wife got back from holiday they invited me to join them at home. It was a very nice place but it was still hard adjusting to living in someone else's house, invading their private spaces. They were really kind and welcoming, encouraging me to "make myself at home", but I had no idea how they expected me to behave while I was there. There were many more new experiences like learning how to work a dishwasher – I hadn't even realised such things existed – and making coffee in a machine. All the food was kept in the fridge and they told me to help myself to whatever I wanted whenever I was hungry, but it was hard to believe that you can just help yourself to food without permission. Sometimes I would be hungry but because they were in the kitchen, reading or talking, I would be too embarrassed to just walk in and help myself to something to eat. Sometimes I would even go out to a café to have a coffee rather than impose on them by making myself one in the house.

I used to work very late into the night and sometimes I wouldn't wake up in the morning as early as they did. There was no pressure to go downstairs to have breakfast with them, and the professor didn't really lay-up breakfast in any formal way, usually just listening to the news on the radio and drinking coffee while working. I think his wife thought I was being a little disrespectful, but actually my problem was that I had too much respect for them to be relaxed enough to behave as I would have done in my own home. It didn't seem right to me that I should sit down and take breakfast with them as if I were an equal in their home.

The whole house was filled with books, more than most of the libraries I had been to in primary schools. It was exciting to be living in a place where there was so much accumulated learning and wisdom. I wanted to read everything and I was painfully aware of how much I still had to learn.

My room was on the third floor, which seemed giddily high for a boy who had grown up sleeping on the bare earth.

I passed my pre-sessional courses with extremely good grades and was then able to start work on my master's degree. There was so much reading and writing involved it took all my energy just to keep up with the other students. Although I could speak English pretty fluently by then my written grammar was still not perfect and I always took longer to write essays than any of the others.

It was a very different experience to Butare. There was never a problem with teachers not turning up and I had to write an essay, and sometimes even two essays, for every lesson that I attended. All the teachers were supportive and inspiring and many of my classmates, seeing that I was struggling with written academic English, offered to help by proof-reading everything for me. But that still meant that I had to go over my work many more times than they had to go over theirs before I felt safe to submit it. It was a gruelling schedule but I managed not to fail at any of the tasks that I was set.

Everyone made me feel welcome and many of them invited me home to meet their families, each one of them different to the others. So much about Western life was surprising to me. I missed my family a lot and my mum didn't have any access to the internet so I couldn't email her. She did, however, have a mobile phone by then, so once a month I would ring her to find out how she was. I emailed Protais a lot and kept in touch with my friends through Facebook and WhatsApp.

Mobile phones had made it Gasharu even though electricity hadn't. So if someone wanted to charge their phone they had to walk to the main road and find someone who was selling charging services. Young people who were lucky enough to get phones would get them charged while they were at school and then talk on them as they walked back and forth across the mountains. My mother had to do the same.

The public relations department at the university was telling the media about my story and that resulted in me being interviewed for the BBC. Once the programme had been broadcast, all sorts of people started contacting the professor, asking if they could offer me a place to stay for part of my time in the country, or asking me to give a talk or an interview.

I stayed with the professor and his wife for about six months and then moved to another family from the Commonwealth Society. They were a retired couple, Christopher and Laurainne, who had lived in Africa for a long time. The man had actually lived in Rwanda for a while when working for an international organisation. They also had a son who was a bit older than me. We went to church together, which hadn't happened with the professor because he and his wife were not religious at all. I still used to go to church on my own when I was with them, finding comfort in the familiarity of the services, a link to my old life.

The professor was very keen on exercise and used to do a lot of cycling and go to the gym at the weekend, but I didn't go with him. He and his wife worked so hard during the week that the weekends were their times together and I respected that. The new family didn't do any sport as they were older. Every day was tightly planned with the professor, but with this family things were much less rigid. I learnt to work on the garden with the wife and I learnt a lot about plants and how to look after them.

I stayed with this family for about three months, but their son was due to visit with the grandchildren, so I then moved to another family who had offered to take me in. This time my hostess was a professor of law, and her home life was different again from the first two. She was a single mother with three children aged between seven and eleven. Her ex-husband lived across the road, so the children would go back and forth. I had no idea how I was meant to behave with the children because I knew that adults in Rwanda behave very differently with their children. I needn't have worried because they loved to play football, so we did that all the time. I always like being with children because they are so honest and straightforward in what they say.

So many things about their life came as a surprise to me. When I saw the mother helping the children with their homework in the evening I would remember how I used to struggle alone to do mine by the light of the fire, or in the morning if I was able to wake myself up early enough. The siblings would also help each other, which was nice to see.

I was learning so much about how different people lived in the West. This family had no scheduled meals at all; they just helped themselves to food whenever they were hungry. In this house I didn't feel too bad about doing this and I started to learn how to cook for myself, buying myself some cookery books. I was twenty-seven years old and only just learning how to cook western food like pasta, or to use a microwave. I also met openly gay people for the first time because in Rwanda that is not a subject that is ever talked about. I had once met an American man who wanted to sleep with me, but that was my only experience. I was very curious to know what their lives were like and whether they suffered any sort of persecution for their lifestyle choice – as they would have done in Rwanda if they had ever had the courage to come out.

There was, and perhaps still is, a perception in Rwanda that all white girls are very open about sex, so all my friends at home assumed that I was dating lots of girls. In reality that wasn't the case and I found the whole business of dating very difficult, puzzling and different from anything I had been brought up with. It was extremely hard for me to understand the signals that girls were giving me. During the course of the year I met a couple of girls who showed an interest, but when they discovered that I intended to go back home to Rwanda at the end of the course they immediately lost their enthusiasm.

Many of the people I confided in were surprised that I would want to go back, assuming that once I had experienced life in Bristol I would not want to return to the African ways. I found that attitude quite offensive. I was actually looking forward to getting back to a more relaxed, less intense and less individualistic life – not to mention a warmer climate.

I was quite surprised by how little some of the students knew about the world outside their own lives. There was one Chinese student on the master's course who didn't know what the word "genocide" meant, although perhaps it was a language problem. It took me some time to get used to the idea that some of the people around me knew nothing about my country or what had happened there.

Even more puzzling was the fact that they expected me to know all about the celebrities and politics of the UK. They would have suffered as much of a culture shock if they had arrived in Gasharu as I had experienced in Geneva.

My own ignorance – or perhaps "innocence" would be a better word – took a different form. At a friend's birthday party someone suggested we should play a game of charades. We all wrote down words on pieces of paper and then everyone had to pick one out and get people to guess what it was without using words. The word I picked out was "vibrator". Since the only thing I knew about vibrating was the phone that Olivia had given me at the bus station, no one could understand my mime at all. In the rules I was allowed to pass it to a friend if I didn't know what it meant. When I did she couldn't stop laughing; such innocence.

While I was in Bristol I did all I could to raise awareness of the genocide and of what was happening in modern Rwanda. I organised an evening to remember the victims of the genocide against the Tutsi and invited around four hundred people, including the High Commissioner of Rwanda to the UK and a number of academics with interests in the area. There were no other Rwandan students at the university at the time that I knew of, just one other girl who was born out there but had been brought to the UK when she was just a few months old. I gave a talk and that was followed by a discussion about genocide denial. The High Commissioner then gave a speech and I handed out pieces of paper, asking people to feel free to write whatever messages they wanted.

A student from Ireland, Saoirse Linda, also invited me to stay with her and her family for a month during the

Christmas holidays at their home in Rostrevor. I found the Irish accent very challenging and almost needed a translator just to go to the pub! On Christmas Day some of locals went swimming in the freezing cold sea, very different to the warm, still waters of Lake Kivu, but I wasn't going to try that. I found the cold weather hard enough to get used to as it was. One evening I gave a talk in Rostrevor's newly opened pub, which was a nice experience, and my friend's family were very generous in supporting me once I had finished my course and gone back to Rwanda to look for a job, which proved to be harder than I had expected.

In my innocence I had imagined that when I came home with my master's degree from England, and my great results from Butare, I would be inundated with job offers. Like many other graduating students around the world I was shocked to find that people didn't automatically want to employ me just because I had been generous enough to offer them my services.

Even though I couldn't find a full-time job, I always managed to find plenty of things to do to fill my time, increase my network of contacts and deepen my knowledge of the world. Because of my journalistic experience at Salus in Butare, I was able to get some commissions from the *New Times*, the only daily paper in Kigali, and I could also do some radio reporting in Kigali at the same time. Apart from being able to improve my English, an extra advantage of working for the *New Times* at the time I was applying for a Masters abroad was that I could go into their offices and take advantage of the free internet connection, allowing me to pursue my job hunt and other networking activities.

For the newspaper I wrote profiles of some blind people and how hard it was to cope as a disabled person in Kigali and how blind girls are exploited by boys. I had become increasingly interested in the subject of equality and I liked finding stories of injustice and then being able to expose it to the light. One of the stories was about Nyange School in the Ngororero District in 1997, where a group of killers came back from the Congo one evening with guns. They burst into a classroom where the students were doing revision and ordered them to divide themselves up into Hutus and Tutsis. The students refused, saying that they were all Rwandans now. Infuriated at being disobeyed, the killers opened fire on all of them, killing seven. Those kids have since become heroes of the reconciliation movement.

The common theme of all my stories, like my dissertation at Butare, seems to be inclusion. They are nearly always about people who are stigmatized by society, which I guess must stem from my having felt so excluded as a small child due to being a Tutsi.

Without a full-time job I had no spare money at all. I had to walk everywhere because I didn't have enough for bus fares, which was very tiring by the end of each day. I still, however, felt that there were opportunities out there for me if I could just pin them down. The important thing was that I should be completely prepared to take advantage of them when they eventually arrived.

Whenever I contacted my American professor in Butare with an update about what I was up to, he was always very encouraging.

"Just keep doing that," he'd say. "You will achieve whatever you want in the end."

20

TALKING AT HARVARD

In Kigali the British Council decided to create a UK/Rwanda alumni group, so I went along to the launch event, never wanting to miss an opportunity to meet new people. Inevitably I got talking to the Country Director, telling her what I was doing, and I sent her a CV afterwards in the hope of perhaps being considered for a job. There was nothing permanent available for me at the time, but they wrote back to say they were going round to universities telling students about the opportunities they were offering for scholarships to the UK and other schemes, and they asked me if I would speak to students about my experiences in England and about finding other ways of getting to the UK.

At the same time, a friend forwarded me an email about an organisation called Arts Connect International based in Boston. They had a resident programme which was calling for applicants who might be "emerging artist leaders of colour". Until that time they had been working with US-based artists but I was intrigued by their mission for inclusion. I thought that if they were truly being inclusive, they should be including artists who were based outside the US. Having nothing to lose, I put in my application, issuing that challenge. They got back to me and I had two interviews.

I told them I also wanted to see what inclusion meant to them! I explained that I use the arts to stop the intergenerational transmission of hatred, and told them that I was planning to set up a foundation.

This was the time when the Black Lives Matter campaign was gaining traction in the US, which helped to make my work topical. They offered me a place and awarded me a grant of $15,000 to stay in Boston for four months between August and December 2016. I was also collaborating with another organisation in New York, which meant I had to go to meet them once a week. I gave talks and seminars talking about my own experiences and how young people and traumatised people can use the arts to address their issues and tell their stories in a peaceful, healing way, just as I had done when I was in school and unable to articulate how I felt in class.

One day I was performing my play at Tuft University, having been invited by Hillel School, and after the performance was over a white student came up to me. She was crying.

"I was planning to kill myself in two days," she told me. "But your play has changed my mind. I will never think again about taking my own life away."

She told me she was going through difficulties but I didn't ask her any more questions, just hugged her and cried with her. It was as intense an experience for me as it was for her, resurrecting so many feelings and emotions from the past.

I nearly always cry when I tell my story to people abroad. I guess it will always be that way. The people I am talking to usually cry too, I think it is because there is something universal about the story, as well as personal. Everyone can identify with it because it was a narrative that involved the whole population of a country. People were either perpetrators of incredible atrocities, victims, onlookers or liberators. No one could remain untouched by the events and by the build-up of hatred that caused them.

Many of the people who heard my story would simply fall silent, unable to think what they should say, lost in their own thoughts as they try to grapple with the reality of what happened. Others hug me. These reactions don't happen so much in Rwanda because survivors still tend not to talk to one another about their experiences. It was terrible for everyone so we do not feel there is anything to be gained from talking about it all the time. To talk about it can be a painful way to relive it. People are wary of asking one another too many personal questions in case they resurrect disturbing memories and traumatise people who are only just managing to hold on to their sanity.

My play, which I was performing to these audiences in America, is about giving people hope. At the end of each performance I give everyone a poem, titled "You Have the Key", and a key for them to unlock the symbolic padlocks which are stopping them from believing in the future, encouraging everyone to become one another's peace. A year later I was still receiving messages from people who had attended those performances, telling me that they still have the keys and wear them round their necks to remind them that there is hope for the future.

One of the venues I we were invited to was Harvard School of Education, to explain what we did as artists to an audience of students who were taking a master's programme in Arts in Education. The students were there either because they were planning to be teachers or professors or because they were going to become artists.

We had to give talks and break into groups according to who wanted to engage in more conversation. The subject of the discussion was "The Aesthetics of Social Change", looking at how we can influence people's attitudes to change, as seen from the perspective of a genocide survivor who was also a sociologist and an artist. I did the same talk at a number of different universities including Taft University, Boston College and University of Massachusetts. I have even done it over Skype.

By aesthetics I was talking about the formal way of influencing people, telling stories and transferring knowledge. The subject is particularly relevant to the black students, who are trained to remain neutral and unemotional when teaching, even if they feel oppressed in their daily lives in America. I was saying that I disagreed with that idea, that I believed that in order to be an effective teacher you needed to be able to show that you are a human being who has feelings and emotions, which can become damaged just like anyone else's. I don't believe you can influence change by staying neutral about racism, particularly if you are, or ever have been, a victim of it.

Among the artists was a young, black American sculptor who made the presentation with me. He came from Missouri, where there are still a lot of racist attitudes. He spoke honestly to the students and he actually cried as he talked about how it felt to be inside a building that had been built by slaves like his grandparents, but which was still not generally accessible to most black students of his generation. Overcome by emotion, he put down the microphone and left the room. In the workshop group some of the students wanted to go and comfort him but I said they should leave him because it was right that he should have been able to speak from the heart and say what he really felt.

They asked me if it was easy to forgive the killers and I explained that it was not easy, but I wanted things to change for future generations and forgiveness was the only possible way of achieving that. If we don't forgive them, what are we going to tell our children? My eyes saw what no child should see, and my ears heard what no child should hear.

21

RECONCILING WITH THE PAST

When I got back to Kigali from America, the Country Director of the British Council emailed to tell me they were thinking about putting together some sort of arts programme and asked if I had any ideas for projects I could do with them. I suggested that I should put together a disability programme for Rwanda. Because of the war between the RPA and the government, as well as the genocide, a larger than normal percentage of our population is disabled in one way or another. Although it is a subject that is talked about in the papers, and laws have been passed by the government, at a practical level there are very few things in place on the ground to help the people who need it the most. They liked the idea and hired me on a part-time basis.

After finishing at Bristol I had sent my CV to many different organisations and universities in pursuit of employment of some sort. One of these organisations was the Aegis Trust, an international organisation working to prevent genocide, honouring the memory of victims and enabling people to meet survivors and learn from their experiences. They are a charity, run from the UK, who have created the Kigali Genocide Museum. I went to their research conference and let them know that I was interested in working with them. They kept sending me opportunities, none of which quite worked out, and eventually they offered me a grant to do research into post-genocide Rwanda, exploring the concept of "re-humanising" the victims. When you have been told for many generations that you are a "cockroach" and that you are "sub-human", it takes time and re-education to restore your confidence.

When I was being hunted as a small child and told that I was a cockroach, I felt that I deserved it. I never wondered why it was happening; I simply accepted that I had to run and hide if I wanted to survive. There were some Tutsis who didn't accept it, who understood the unfairness of it and fought back before they were killed. Most, however, were like me and my family and resigned themselves to the fact that being brutally slaughtered was their inevitable fate if they were captured. All I was thinking about during those years was how to live for one more day, or one more hour, before my destiny caught up with me and I was captured and killed.

When I go back to the village now many of the killers have now returned, having either escaped punishment or served their prison sentences. They greet me as if none of the killings ever happened, as if we had grown up together in the normal way, without any interruption. Sometimes there have been family problems when killers return, after having been away for many years, and find that their wives have given birth to children by other men. There have been cases of women and children being beaten and killed as a result of such perceived betrayals and jealousy.

"Ah, you are such a grown-up man now," these neighbours say as they embrace me. "You are becoming so like your father." And at that moment I remember that the man with his arms around me may well have participated in the murder of my father, and I wonder how he can talk so casually about a man who was so mistreated by his community.

Sometimes survivors find it impossible to stay silent under these circumstances, and they blurt out something in anger, letting the bitterness burst through the pretence, but I tend to keep the sadness inside me because there is nothing to be gained from constantly re-opening old wounds. In many ways our family was lucky because so many of us did survive. I know of many families that were completely wiped out. I am also able to leave the village when I want to, returning to the more anonymous city life in Kigali, where the memories are not so intense or so personal.

I still have nightmares filled with the blood and the smells of exhumed bodies, with the sounds of hunters whooping with excitement and crashing through the undergrowth as they pursue me, expecting them to kill me at any moment as I jump over or hide beneath the piles of dead bodies. I still have dreams of my father coming to me to talk. I still lock all the doors whenever I am inside a house, and when I take a shower I keep my eyes open all the time.

I have started a foundation to help young people to find their way in the world. Remembering back to when I was fifteen and so angry that I planned to become a killer, I think that if I had not been lucky enough to find teachers who believed in me, inspired me, gave me hope and showed me the right way to go, things would have turned out very differently. I would be someone else; a killer, a criminal and quite probably already dead. Through my foundation I want to use the arts to help young people to find the strength needed to achieve their potential and unpack their dreams.

In 2016 I was walking from Gasharu to the church, following the paths that my feet knew so well from the past, and I was suddenly aware that I was doing it as a free man. No one was hunting me. There was no one and nothing that I had to hide from anymore. I felt that I was walking in hope rather than in fear.

I thought of all the people of my age or younger who might still be walking in fear and anger, as I had done during the months when I went back every day to be where my father had fallen for the last time, and before that when I was trying to stay alive one day at a time. I wanted to think of things that I could do to show these people that there is hope. I decided that I would plan a hundred-day walk across all the districts of Rwanda, giving talks and sleeping at the former killing sites like the churches, the schools and the mass graves, to show people that there was hope, that it was safe, that there was no need to fear things any more. I committed to do the walk on the twenty-fifth anniversary of the genocide in 2019. People gave me food and shelter when I needed it and I was joined and supported by people from all over the world, particularly Dylan Cuddy from the USA, who volunteered to walk with me, taking photos and videos. I covered each of Rwanda's thirty districts over the hundred days, one day for each of the days that the massacre took place. I planted trees, visited care homes for the disabled and elderly, ran food and clothing drives, met survivors and perpetrators, walked and played football with the children of Rwanda.

Life in Gasharu is much the same today as it was when I was a child, although more people now wear shoes as they trudge through the mountains in search of food, water and education. My primary school now has a few more classrooms built from brick and a proper toilet block, but the children running around outside look much the same as us, their ancestors. Despite the poverty in Rwanda, however, there is no other country where I would want to live permanently. It is my true homeland, a beautiful country with infinite possibilities for the future.

Sometimes my mother tells me or my brother that we remind her of my father in the way we laugh or the way we walk, or because we are working hard. All my sisters have something about their faces that reminds us of him. Sometimes one of the songs that he loved to sing will come on the radio and I can see that it brings back memories for her as well as for us. We talk about him a lot in the family. I think Mum loved him very deeply.

My brother, Protais, studied botany and conservation at university and now works in the Nyungwe rainforest for an American organisation called the Wildlife Conservation Society. He has married and has started a family. Being three years older than me, and being able to understand more about what was happening to us during those months, I think the effects may have been worse for him at the time. He has also been living and working in

166

the same part of the country, living amongst the same people and the same memories, while I have been away in the UK, America, Butare and Kigali. He knew more about what was happening when the killers started returning from prison and threatening our mother. So in many ways the genocide against the Tutsi has been a worse experience for him than it was for me.

With the help of many of the people I met in the UK, Protais, my sisters and I have managed to make enough money to build our mother a house with concrete floors and a blue tin roof, which is close enough to the main road to receive some power and water, and surrounded with enough land for her to grow most of the food she needs.

People who grow old in our village are very vulnerable. Should someone fall sick there is no hope that an ambulance would be able to get to them. Several of the neighbours would have to get together to build a stretcher in order to carry the patient on their shoulders all the way to the main road, which would be a long and difficult journey. Although there is a cheap health insurance, "mutuelle de santé" that has done a lot of good for Rwandans, we feel better now that we know our mum could be reached more easily in an emergency.

She still cooks outside on an open fire, but she no longer shares the indoor rooms with her livestock and now she even has a cow of her own. Initially she didn't like drinking milk, but we have persuaded her to try, starting out by putting sugar in it to make it more palatable, and she is coming round to it. Now she is quite fancy and even wears some shoes and clothes that I bought for her in the UK. To people in the West it would seem like a very modest house, but I think if my father was still alive to share it with her, he would be telling everyone, especially once he had some banana beer inside him, that he had been right all along and that his children had made him a rich man.

ABOUT THE AUTHORS

Hyppolite Ntigurirwa is an artist, activist, and founder of Be the Peace, an organisation focusing on the use of art to halt the intergenerational transmission of hate and to promote the power of cross-generational healing.

A child survivor of the 1994 genocide against the Tutsi, Hyppolite continues to promote reconciliation and peace throughout Rwanda. In 2019, he envisioned and conducted the "Be the Peace Walk," a 100-day walk performance piece in which he walked across the country in commemoration of 25 years since the end of the genocide.

Hyppolite is an alumnus of Yale World Fellows Programme and a 2020/2021 Research Fellow at Schell Centre for International Human Rights at Yale University. Hyppolite was an international Artist in Residence with Arts Connect International in Boston in 2016. Since then he has worked as Arts Program Manager for the British

Council in Rwanda, focusing on disability rights and societal inclusion until August 2020. He is a Peace Ambassador for One Young World, Peace Scholar and his work has been covered by global media including BBC, NPR, SABC, and Dutchwelle.

Andrew Crofts is a ghostwriter and author who has published more than a hundred books, both fiction and non-fiction, a dozen of which were *Sunday Times* number one bestsellers.

Andrew's name first became known among publishers for the stories he brought them by the otherwise disenfranchised. Travelling all over the world he worked with victims of enforced marriages in North Africa and the Middle East, sex workers in the Far East, orphans in war-torn areas like Croatia and dictatorships like Romania, victims of crimes and abused children everywhere.

The success of these books brought many very different people to his door; first came the celebrities from the worlds of film, music, television and sport, and then the real elite in the form of world leaders in business and politics.

Andrew has also published his own fiction, most recently "What Lies Around Us" and "Secrets of the Italian Gardener", which both draw on his experiences ghostwriting for the powerful and wealthy.

His books on writing include "Ghostwriting" (A&C Black) and "The Freelance Writer's Handbook" (Piatkus), which has been reprinted eight times over twenty years and "Confessions of a Ghostwriter" (Friday Project).

Printed in Great Britain
by Amazon